Praise for *Anothe*

"Get ready for a journey of keen awareness of the opposites in life that often reside in the same space: being fragile yet strong, fearful but unafraid, broken yet healing, lost while discovering self. Filled with stories of adventure that helped one woman navigate heartbreaking loss, *Another Step Up the Mountain* teaches us how fragile life is, yet is a shining example of how fearlessly living life on the edge connects us with the world and our inner selves and, ultimately, leads to healing."

—**Marshall Ulrich**, adventurer and bestselling author of *Running on Empty* and *Both Feet on the Ground*

"What a ride! In *Another Step Up the Mountain*, Dianette takes you to the top of the world and the depths of the soul as she reminds us every day is training day for the challenges, sorrow, boundless joy, and intense beauty that true adventure and the search for meaning and purpose bring. Biting wit and gallows humor combined with compassion and heart—Dianette and her story will help get you up and down any mountain."

—**Kelly Chapman Meyer**, founder of OneSun Farms

"Adventure racing and climbing Everest gave me a real appreciation for Dianette's mental tenacity and physical endurance. *Another Step Up the Mountain* is her personal spiritual journey that she willingly shares with us.

Climbing the highest mountain in Antarctica with Johnny Strange when he was twelve and bumping into him at the North Pole years later gives me a unique perspective on him. We spoke of passion and risk, and how he wanted to live his life as fully as possible. With their shared 'Life Wish' ever present, *Another Step Up the Mountain* is truly a love story."

—**Vern Tejas**, mountain guide

"No one I know has the courage to explore the world and the limits of herself. A must read!"

—**Gerald W. Abrams**, executive producer

"I really loved the book—so impressive! I am humbled. *Another Step Up the Mountain* beautifully illustrates the resilience with which Dianette approached each challenge in her life."

—**Mary Gadams**, founder of Racing The Planet

"Dianette's life is rife with summits and valleys, and completing this book is a testament to living her truth—*Another Step Up the Mountain*."

—**Laureen Nolan Sills**, founder of Malibu Special Education Foundation

"Dianette is a force of nature. Whether she's climbing the highest mountains or tackling the massive challenge of writing a book, she tells her story of triumph and tragedy with style and courage. What a fantastic achievement."

—**John Watkin**, Emmy-winning producer/director

"Dianette Wells is truly magical. I've seen her in action as a wonderful mother and friend. We can all learn from her tenacity, humanity, and endurance."

—**Tara Sutphen**, world-renowned hypnotherapist, psychic, author, and radio host

"In *Another Step Up the Mountain,* Dianette candidly shares adversities that she faced while pursuing her passion for extreme sports. When her son tragically died in a wingsuiting accident, she withdrew until her enthusiasm for racing and mountaineering helped her through the loss.

"It's an incredible true story of adventure, adversity, challenges, coping with the loss of a son, and of how one can overcome the darkest moments in your life! A must read!"

—**Harald Zundel**, professional adventure racer, United States Navy SEAL Officer (1994–1998) Lieutenant, SEAL Team Three

"This is a must-read for any athlete mother who is torn between the desire to compete and the guilt that comes from leaving young children at home to race. Dianette openly shares her struggle to be the perfect mom, ideal wife, and reliable teammate, and she invites us into her lived experience to find out whether being everything to everyone is even possible without losing yourself. She explores the highly controversial topic of what risks are acceptable for mothers and how those same pursuits are viewed so differently for fathers.

"Not many will know the devastating loss of a child—and I don't wish that for any mother—but if you do find yourself a member of our club, know that you too can survive the unthinkable. We will be remembering our children in the brightest shooting star above Mt. Kilimanjaro, the shimmer of a water droplet down a limestone cavern in the Grand Canyon, the tiny desert flowers on Mt. San Jacinto, the summit of every mountain we have climbed together, and appreciate each breath we take on this incredible planet with Johnny and Emory in our hearts."

—**Tricia Middleton**, Eco-Challenge race producer and mother to Aiden, Camryn, Emory and Nolan

"Johnny Strange was my best friend, and the toughest, most determined person I've ever had the blessing to know. It wasn't until I got older that I realized the type of mother it took to raise such a strong, determined, skilled individual. Dianette is the definition of strong, determined, and relentless. Describing Dianette as inspiring is a large understatement. She has experienced and endured more than most people could ever comprehend, and lives to tell about it."

—**Trevor Jacob**, Olympic snowboarder and entrepreneur

"Dianette is fearless, tireless, relentless, demonstrating what can be achieved with her breathtaking accomplishments, and invites others to join and participate—changing lives by getting them to push past perceived barriers towards high adventure!"

—**Nicholas Kent** and **Julie Berk**, entertainment marketing executives

"*Another Step Up the Mountain* has captured what life is like for extreme athlete Dianette Wells as she and her family look to max out life on the edge. Her children have followed along, ever entwined with all her adventures. Her son Johnny shared that same dream and passion and lived on that edge. Dianette shares her story of the highs and lows in the struggle to reach the summit of life. She inspires us all to never lose focus on that summit, even when it's not always visible. She challenges you to leave hope behind and find the reality of success or failure. This journey will take you to some of the lows Dianette experienced and battled through in her life living on the edge, but one thing's for certain: the only way to reach the tallest summit is to take *Another Step Up the Mountain*!"

—**Blain Reeves**, US Army best ranger competition winner, Beast of the East Adventure Race solo champion, road cycling champion, ultra-marathoner, Eco Challenge 95, 96, 97, 19

ANOTHER STEP UP THE MOUNTAIN

Books by Brit Elders

A Happy Move: Everything You Need to Know Before and After the Boxes Are Packed, Beyond Words, 2024

UFO…Contact from the Pleiades, 45th Anniversary Edition, Beyond Words, 2024

Expeditions: Gold, Shamans and Green Fire, Wakani North LLC, 2013

ANOTHER STEP UP
THE MOUNTAIN

A Journey of Courage

Dianette Wells with Brit Elders

mango
PUBLISHING
CORAL GABLES

For permission requests, please contact the publisher at:
Mango Publishing Group
2850 S Douglas Road, 2nd Floor
Coral Gables, FL 33134 USA
info@mango.bz

For special orders, quantity sales, course adoptions and corporate sales, please email the
publisher at sales@mango.bz. For trade and wholesale sales, please contact Ingram Publisher
Services at customer.service@ingramcontent.com or +1.800.509.4887.

Another Step Up the Mountain: A Journey of Courage

Library of Congress Cataloging-in-Publication number: 2023952619
ISBN: (paperback) 978-1-68481-677-4, (eBook) 978-1-68481-543-2
BISAC category code:BIO026000, BIOGRAPHY & AUTOBIOGRAPHY / Personal Memoirs

This book is dedicated to my mom, Gladys Farnham,
who worked harder than any woman I know; to my twin brother,
Fred, the human who has known me and been with me the longest;
and, most importantly, to the three amazing humans I'm privileged
to call mine. Thank you for choosing me to be your mom.
I love you bigger than the universe, times ten.

Dianette Wells personal collection

Table of Contents

Foreword

Adventure. It's a word that stirs the soul, ignites the imagination, and beckons us to venture beyond our comfort zones. In the world of adventure, there are those who tiptoe on the periphery, dabbling in adrenaline-fueled activities when the mood strikes. And then there are those who plunge headfirst into the heart-pounding unknown, embracing life's wild side with unwavering courage and boundless determination. The story you are about to embark upon is testament to the latter. It's a tale of a remarkable woman, a modern-day explorer who has chosen to dance on the razor's edge of life, engaging in adventure sports that push the limits of human endurance and daring.

From a comfortable life as a Malibu housewife, to racing through the jungles of Borneo and Fiji and the glaciers of New Zealand, to climbing the Seven Summits, Dianette Wells transformed her life through sports. It began when I introduced her to my expedition competition, the Eco-Challenge, and it was the catalyst for the next two decades of her life.

I've had the privilege of witnessing countless adventures in my career as an adventure series producer. I've seen ordinary people discover the extraordinary within themselves when faced with the unknown. Yet Dianette's journey is unique, and her spirit indomitable. As you read these pages, you'll travel with her, experiencing the excitement and challenges she faced as she ventured into nature's most formidable forces—towering mountains, raging storms, and unforgiving deserts.

But this book is more than just a chronicle of daring feats. It's a heartfelt journey of self-discovery rooted in a passion for sports, the emotional trauma of divorce that many experience, and the devastating, unexpected loss of her only son. *Another Step Up the Mountain* is a celebration of the human spirit's boundless capacity for courage and resilience, even during the most tragic of events. Dianette's journey reminds us that life's greatest rewards often lie beyond the boundaries of our comfort zones, waiting for those willing to reach out and grasp them.

As you turn these pages, you will be inspired by Dianette's unwavering determination, her unrelenting pursuit of the extraordinary, and her unshakeable belief that the world is a vast playground meant to be explored to its fullest. So gear up, dear reader, for the adventure of a lifetime, and prepare to be captivated by the incredible story that unfolds—a story that proves that, in the end, it's not the destination, but the journey itself that defines us.

Mark Burnett
Emmy Award-winning producer and former chairman of MGM
Park City, Utah

Preface

2015

I was compelled to look—no—to stare at the latest photo Johnny had posted of himself wingsuiting in Switzerland. Beneath it was the caption, "Carving down the mountain today in my Jedei 2 #wingsuit #HyperDrive."

He was flying so close to the treetops that it seemed as though he could have reached out and touched them. The sky was clear and blue, and his black and red wingsuit contrasted against the gray of the sharp granite cliff behind him. His black, full-face helmet held his GoPro in front of it. He was perfectly horizontal, flying, arms spread out like a soaring bird. I couldn't stop staring at that photo.

Wingsuiting isn't something you wake up and decide to do one day. It's a long progression of learning and experience. For Johnny, it started with skydiving. That was something he'd begged his father and me to let him do since he was little. He'd been paragliding since he was fourteen and an avid skydiver once he turned eighteen. It was fun to a point, but there was always a next level to investigate and attempt.

For Johnny, that next level was BASE (building, antenna, span, and earth) jumping, which you only do after a certain number of jumps from an airplane. The next step up the progressive ladder of danger is wearing a wingsuit and jumping from an airplane for a certain number of jumps. Then one must learn how to fly while wearing the suit. That requires jumping from a hot-air balloon, provided you can get access to one. Johnny had wrangled time in a hot-air balloon for that very purpose. You continue to practice and perfect your skills in the wingsuit until, years later, you literally fly from the edge of a cliff. Even the intense rush or thrill or skill of sailing off a cliff face isn't always enough. It wasn't nearly enough for Johnny.

He took it a step further. Proximity wingsuiting is seeing just how close you can get to other objects, like trees, waterfalls, and cliffs, while flying by them at over a hundred mph. This is what gave BASE jumpers an even bigger thrill, an even greater sense of speed. The closer you were to the object, the more you felt the speed, and the less chance there was to correct any error.

The photo was jarring. I was used to seeing photos and videos of him leaping out of airplanes and helicopters, from hot-air balloons and bridges. I had never seen my son this close to the ground. This was something different. This was proximity wingsuit BASE jumping.

––––––––

Normally, when I wake up, the first thing I do is look at my cell phone. I didn't on the morning of October 1, 2015, because the day before I had dropped the phone into a toilet. It was sitting in a bag of rice, drying out, when I grabbed it as I walked out the door. I was feeling happy, content. I was forty-nine and had three remarkable children who were settling into their own lives. I was an independent divorced woman with a boyfriend and no plans to marry again.

I got into my car, plugged my phone into the USB not knowing whether or not it would work, and started the thirty-five-minute drive to my home in Park City, Utah. Ten minutes into the drive, a call came over my Bluetooth.

I recognized the number. It was my ex-husband's landline in Malibu. My brain went into hyperdrive. It couldn't be either of my daughters. Ella was just arriving home in New York from her mini honeymoon. Olivia was also on the East Coast. None of the kids were in Malibu, which was an hour behind my time zone. Why would my ex be calling me at seven thirty in the morning Pacific Time?

I instinctively knew that I didn't want to know. "Why are you calling me?" I demanded.

"Johnny," is all he could say.

"Oh my God, I forgot to renew his Global Rescue insurance. This is going to cost a lot of money to get him home on a medical flight," I rambled, trying to will that scenario into reality.

"No," he started.

I don't remember the rest of what he said.

Introduction

W ould you risk everything, including death, in order to feel fully alive? Or would you stick to the safe trail, following the reliable, worn path of others? To be clear, I'm asking if you would truly gamble with your one precious life in order to be fulfilled emotionally and spiritually. If you answered yes to this question, would you also allow your friends, loved ones, and children the same grace in choosing their own unique path? If you answered no, then this book may change your mind.

I met Dianette in 1999, before the Eco-Challenge in Borneo. Both of our teams were being featured by CBS's *48 Hours* in a primetime special. Dianette and her husband had a complicated relationship, and that made for good television. I was eight years clean and sober, which also makes for good TV, and I was still trying to find my way as a husband and father. Frankly, I think we were both way over our heads in this race, trying to be brave but more than a little freaked out by the scope of this challenge, not to mention the great likelihood that we would make fools of ourselves on national television. As it turned out, we learned that we were both tougher than we could have imagined. We survived the race and learned some kick-ass lessons. More importantly, we became friends.

We started to do some training together, and even discussed being teammates someday.

We met each other's kids, and we all got together a few times for some fun and adventure. I loved Dianette's children for their energy and kindness. As a mom, Dianette was a beautiful combination of cheerleader and taskmaster. Her deep devotion to her kids was matched only by her tenacity as an athlete.

For Dianette, it wasn't a question of making a choice between her kids and her passion for adventure. She wanted both and saw no reason she couldn't be a great mother and a dedicated adventurer. She proved that a mother isn't required to give up her own dreams in order to be a good parent. Whether she meant to or not, she also gave her kids a powerful role model to follow. Each of them mimicked her passion and drive in their own ways. In particular, her son Johnny was a uniquely focused and single-minded soul.

My two sons, Brett and Kevin, took an instant liking to Johnny. They wanted to learn to surf and hike and climb like Johnny. They envied his freewheeling nature and his overpowering drive, which often meant that he got his way. I jokingly told my kids that they needed to learn to sell their ideas better, like Johnny did. He simply wouldn't take no for an answer.

After Borneo, Dianette and I teamed up for adventure races in Vietnam and Fiji. We also raced as teammates at the RAAM (Race Across America) bike race. We loved racing together, and our teams were successful. But our success was about more than winning. When you run through the fire with someone, the bonds that are created become unbreakable. The constant pushing is equal parts self-discovery and self-abuse. We had fun, but neither of us ever lost sight of the inherent value of cultural exploration and self-imposed hardship.

As teammates, the thing I remember most is the laughter. It's a really absurd sport that forces a kind of suffering that's hard to replicate anywhere else in life. Laughing at ourselves made it tolerable. Probably the only reason I was any good at adventure racing was because I had honed my sleep deprivation skills as a cocaine addict for ten years. This is not recommended training, but it worked out for me.

Around 2004, Dianette turned her attention to climbing big mountains, and I partnered with Matt Damon to make a film about my expedition across the Sahara Desert (*Running the Sahara*), running nearly five thousand miles from Senegal to the Red Sea. I kept running toward my goals and she kept climbing toward hers. But we never lost touch, never lost the bond created through shared misery. Though we went our own ways, our mutual passion for adventure and our equally dark and twisted senses of humor assured our friendship would survive any challenge.

Then my world fell apart, and our friendship was tested. Many of my friends abandoned me—but not Dianette. Instead of shying away, she stepped up for me, helping to look after my kids, encouraging me at every turn, channeling my anger at the unfairness of the situation, and fiercely defending me.

Dianette was there for me when I needed her, and I vowed to always do the same for her. In this regard, I could not keep my promise. I wanted to, but it just wasn't possible. When Dianette's world crumbled, I'm not sure anyone or anything could have relieved that pain. All pain is not equal. Some pain can't be managed or fixed or tamped down. It just has to be survived. While she tried to accept the love and help of others, she mostly compartmentalized her pain and suffered in private.

This book is a deep and thoughtful examination of triumph and tragedy. Dianette opens up her life to us in the most vulnerable ways. She has spent years trying to reconcile the disparities of her dual existence. On one hand, she felt the unstoppable pull of extreme adventure and the edgy excitement of dancing on the razor's edge. On the other hand, she wanted to try being normal, to start a family, to be a "traditional" wife. She hoped to take care of her kids in ways that she herself never experienced as a child. This internal conflict caused serious personal damage through eating disorders and emotional trauma in her marriage. However, it was this buttoned-up home life that pushed Dianette to seek utter freedom in the wild, which in turn drove her guilt over not being the perfect mother. This cycle was unsustainable, causing each side of her life to feed the other until the pressure grew too great, causing the whole structure to collapse.

Dianette's story lifts us up and breaks our hearts all at once. For me, the lesson here is clear. We share our lives *with* our kids. We don't live *for* them and they don't live *for* us. Each of us must try to live our best life as an individual, separate and apart from everyone else, including our children. At our best, as parents, we share our vulnerabilities and fears with our kids, letting them know that we are not perfect and that everything will work out. In the end, all we can do is to love and support our children, even when their choices terrify us.

Charlie Engle
Author of *Running Man*, Scribner
Addiction recovery coach
Ultra endurance athlete

Chapter 1
1998

Dianette hiking

I *want to climb that*, I thought to myself, as I looked out the car window to the towering spires of Mount Whitney, the highest peak in the contiguous United States. Whoa, that thought came out of nowhere. I was a cheerleader, not an outdoorsy, camping, mountaineer type. Granola and Birkenstocks were a hard pass for me. Yet, something deep inside me was instantly attracted to those peaks.

I recalled seeing Mount Whitney's spires for the first time as a teenager. My boyfriend and I were headed to Mammoth Mountain to go skiing. I felt so cool as we tooled up the highway in his red Mazda RX-7, seemingly without a care in the world. I looked forward to those few days when I could escape my job, school, and the alcoholic home environment in which I existed. Then I looked over and saw the towering spires and the summit of Mount Whitney. I recognized that it was something special and knew that someday I would climb it, but beyond that I didn't give much thought to it. This magnificent mountain seemed to beckon me to it. I couldn't explain the feeling I had then—and I can't explain it now—but somehow, deep down inside, I knew that I would one day climb that imposing peak.

A decade later, my husband and I made that same trek to Mammoth to ski and, as the magnificent rocky spires came into view, I again thought, *I'm going to climb that.*

This time the feeling was different than it was when I was sixteen. It wasn't a distant goal for an undefined time in the future. The concept of climbing Whitney felt as if it was getting closer to being a reality. I silently stared, mesmerized by the craggy range, then realized that I was smiling at the possibility. I must have verbalized that I wanted to climb Whitney, because my husband's voice interrupted my thought as he explained how he and his law school buddies had ascended it while they were in their twenties. He made it sound like a really great time, but he didn't offer to climb it with me. I assumed that his lack of encouragement was because he'd already done it, or maybe because it was so hard, he didn't want to ever do it again. I wasn't sure why he wasn't more supportive and felt a bit frustrated by his overt avoidance of my comment. With a building sense of frustration, I silently turned my attention back to the mountain.

Driving up Highway 395, Whitney looks like a line of enormous rock spires that are often enveloped in a misty haze. The buttes were like a magnet that drew me to them. I didn't know why. I didn't know a thing about climbing and had never considered climbing anything, much less this treacherous-looking part of the Sierra Nevada. Yet, somehow, I knew in the core of my being that I would stand at its pinnacle. With that inner knowledge, I discovered an uncanny peace and calmness that's created by something you desire when there is no doubt in your soul that it will happen—when the time is right.

The exhilaration of Whitney's assent was in the future because, at that moment, my very existence was centered on my husband and my three incredible children, their activities, and remodeling our Malibu home. I had a degree in business management, but I felt more complete being a full-time stay-at-home mom, which I loved and am grateful to have been. I wanted our home to be the household on the block where all the neighborhood kids came to play, something that was reminiscent of the Kool-Aid commercials I had seen as a child. As a kid, I came home to an empty house because my mom was a single parent, working full-time as a nurse, and, as much as I appreciated her working so hard to keep our family together, I wanted to be there for my kids when they came home from school.

I had other dreams, too. I had studied to become a CPA, wanted to be a successful businesswoman early in life, and had received my degree after our first child was born. I've always had multiple goals for myself, but sometimes one must take precedence over another. Being pulled in two very different directions can be frustrating when the two objectives don't always merge well. I never looked back wondering "what if," and never regretted choosing to be there for my young children.

I had married when I was twenty-three, and had a baby when I was twenty-four, another at the age of twenty-five, and another when I was thirty.

Although I tried to be everything my husband wanted in a wife, I couldn't. He wanted me to be at home with the kids, seeing to their needs and his, yet he wanted a carefree party wife like those some of his friends bragged about. To me, that was a contradiction. Oh, and he felt I should have an income. To him no income meant I had no opinion on things, no voice. I was too busy chasing after back-to-back toddlers, running the house, and managing our lifestyle, which he charted, to be very spontaneous. Our children were everything to me. Ella, the oldest, was goal-oriented and studious. She was sweet, logical, and smart. Her dreams were very grounded and realistic, and she was never as wild as our middle child, Johnny.

Johnny had no fear. By the time he was two, his favorite activity was energetically climbing anything taller than he was and soaring from one piece of furniture to another. While catapulting from a chair in our bedroom to the bed, he misjudged the distance and came crashing down on the bed frame. Blood gushed from his forehead as I dialed 911.

While we waited in a room at the hospital for the doctor, Johnny, despite his injury, wasn't slowing down one bit. Running full speed around the gurney, he tripped and fell on something sharp near the wheel. That little mishap resulted in more blood and another set of stitches in his forehead.

Eight days later, he proudly announced that he could fly and, while proving it by jumping off a chair in the living room, he scored yet another set of stitches. Pros by this point, we didn't panic and emergency personnel weren't called. We calmly drove him back to St. John's Hospital, where we found the same people we'd seen on our last visit sitting behind the admitting desk. I turned to my husband and said, "They are going to report us to Child Services."

I felt slightly terrified when he replied, "I know."

Johnny was strapped into a papoose board to limit his movement and stabilize him for the stitches. He cried, and my heart broke. I wanted so badly to take away the pain and fear. We were asked to leave the room as his forehead was sutured up once again. All three of us were traumatized by the results of his aerial acrobatics. When the doctor finished and invited us back into the room, I asked if she thought there was something mentally wrong with our son. Our oldest daughter, Ella, had never had so much as a scratch but, in less than two weeks, Johnny had received three sets of stitches adorning his forehead. The doctor looked up and smiled. "He's a boy," she replied. "Get used to it. I have boys. Buy him a helmet."

For the rest of his childhood, I prayed daily that he would safely get to the age of eighteen.

It wasn't long after the flying incidents that my husband bought Johnny a surfboard despite having declared, while Johnny was still in the womb, that no son of his was going to be a surf bum. I stood there shaking my head as I watched my three-year-old son walking side-by-side with his father, carrying a used surfboard out of Becker Surf. It was another tool to aid Johnny's constant testing and pushing of limits. By the age of four, he declared that he wanted to hang out of helicopters and take photographs when he grew up, but in the meantime, he was content to stand on the bow of a boat, arms out, face turned to the sun, with the wind blowing past him. It was a sensation he loved because he felt like he was flying.

After our third child, Olivia, came along, I was still content being a stay-at-home mother, but the relationship with my husband, who was ten years my senior, was strained. He expected me to be a stay-at-home mom, yet he would say things that demonstrated he had no respect for what I provided and accomplished daily—or for me. He'd tell me I needed to "contribute to the family" or to "get a job." He had no clue of what I was contributing to the family and that being a full-time mom is a job.

There were times when he would suddenly stop speaking to me for days. I couldn't understand how we could lovingly say goodnight to each other and in the morning, I would be met with cold silence. I didn't understand the inconsistencies of his mood swings, nor did I feel they were warranted. I had relinquished almost all control over my life in order to live up to his concept of a dutiful wife. I had zero authority over our finances and was blocked from making any contributions to the decision-making processes for the family. I had no career and had intentionally chosen not to seek one. My life was centered on the children, the home, and my workouts at the local gym, where I had fortunately connected with other moms.

Gym time was important to me, not just because of the camaraderie, but also because it helped control my weight, which, at that time, I felt was the only aspect in my life that I effectively dominated. Because of my need to restrict my weight, I developed anorexia and bulimia, and was so driven to strive for certain numbers on the scale that it became a way of life.

The first time I forced myself to throw up, I was actually proud of myself. I closed the door to our bedroom and locked it. Then I walked into our bathroom and locked that door as well. Alone in my bathroom, I shoved two fingers down my throat. In the act of purging, I finally felt successful at something. I realized that, for me at that time, I was using it as a way to release stress in my life. I felt I had discovered a new tool that I could use to deal with the emotional pressure I was living under.

With this new ability, I could eat normally and not gain a pound. My husband could have the perfectly thin wife he wanted. He made me feel fat by constantly reinforcing that he liked thin women, and openly joked that we should have had a pre-nuptial agreement stating that I couldn't gain x number of pounds. When I hit 101 pounds, he again reminded me how much he liked thin women and cruelly stated that, if I ever gained weight, he would divorce me. My weight, and what I did or didn't eat, was my decision. It was the only thing in my life I thought I controlled.

I couldn't be thin enough for him. I was never going to be enough for him. Even though I was actually not at all overweight, I ceded to his ideals, criticisms, and the threat of divorce. Looking back, my purging wasn't to give him power; it was to have some power of my own. I didn't realize that what I thought I controlled was actually fueling his vision of the perfect wife. Because of my self-imposed food restrictions, while I was trying to get pregnant with Olivia, it took me a year to succeed because I was so thin. Once she was born,

I returned to the old bad habits of using purges to preserve some form of dominance over my life and my ninety-nine-pound weight.

I felt like an outright failure when I gained a pound. At one point, my head was bigger than my body and, even though I recognized that as a fact, it didn't matter. I just wanted the scale to read ninety-nine pounds. That was the goal that I strove to achieve and maintain.

I knew most of my Malibu friends from my children's school, from the local gym, or my moms' workout group. Most of us were in great shape, and it didn't hurt that our little city was a rural, outdoor destination. Right after school drop-offs were completed, we headed to the gym almost every day, or rode bikes, hiked all over the hills in Southern California, or surfed. Surrounded by mountains and ocean, you have to try hard not to do anything physical when you live there.

One day at the gym, I mentioned that I wanted to climb Mount Whitney. One friend volunteered to climb with me, and before long, eleven of us had decided to make the trek up the mountain. I was practically euphoric: I was going to live my dream of climbing Whitney! While I hated leaving the kids, I looked forward to the respite from my husband. I rationalized the inner contradiction I was feeling by saying it would only be two nights, and I would be home early on the third day.

The anticipation of attempting the summit and not knowing the outcome brought up a sense of exhilaration that I had never felt before. Maybe it was naiveté or the thrill of expectation, but for some reason we all felt capable of ascending the mountain, even though we had no real concept of the scope of the project. There were no training regimens or advice from the internet in 1998—at least none that I knew of. We all just went along with the idea of climbing Whitney, blissfully not knowing what we didn't know. I hadn't read much about Mount Whitney and didn't know a thing about climbing, but, collectively, we knew enough to stuff our packs with food, water, warm clothes, and probably a lot of things we didn't even need.

Our group of moms and friends included Georgeann Nichols, a lawyer, ballroom dancer, and spin teacher; Debbie Felman, Malibu's famous aerobics instructor; a doctor's wife; the oldest of the group, Nan Gail, who at the time was the wife of actor Max Gail, famous for his role in the series *Barney Miller*; Alicia Nelson, the youngest of the group and a trainer at Malibu Fitness; Dale Schaffer, who was also a dedicated Malibu Fitness attendee and a top-notch lawyer; Laureen Sills, a woman with a delightful sense of humor and another mom of three; Tracy Murgatroyd, who never turned down an adventure; and Laura Rosenthal, a therapist who was always there when you needed her.

We drove north in four cars to the Dow Villas Motel in Lone Pine, California. Lone Pine is a small town (population 1,484, elevation 3,700 feet). This is where most people climbing Mount Whitney choose to stay. A sharp left off the 395, just past our motel, takes one up the windy steep road to the trailhead of Whitney. This area is known as the Whitney Portal, and there's a rustic little store there with a café that makes excellent cheeseburgers. Some of us went there after we first arrived in Lone Pine. It's a great place to hang out for an hour or two, have a bite to eat, and let your body acclimatize to the eight-thousand-foot elevation. We were all coming from sea level and we knew that climbing to 14,505 feet would be a bit of a shock to our bodies. As a skier, I was accustomed to the change of elevation, as were some of the others. We knew that climbing would be more difficult than skiing and that taking some time to adapt to the higher elevation would be beneficial.

We returned to the motel and agreed to meet later for an early dinner. After dinner at the pizza place across the street from the motel and a quick trip to the little convenience market on the corner, we tried to get a few hours of sleep before our three a.m. start time from the trailhead.

We left the parking lot of the Dow Villas in the middle of the night. It was a bit chilly, but not as cold as it would be at the trailhead. Our four cars followed close together for the twenty-minute drive up to the portal parking lot, which was half-empty.

As we emerged from our warm cars, the illumination from our headlamps helped us find the trailhead that we had visited the previous afternoon. I could feel butterflies in my stomach as my anticipation grew. I asked myself if it was the excitement of the climb, or just jitters. I couldn't help but grin when I saw Laureen Sills in her pearls. Nan Gail was nicely decked out in a cute outfit, and Tracy Murgatroyd and Dale Schaffer had great pieces of new gear.

Although we had agreed to partner up, the whole group stayed together for the first couple of hours. The buddy system was a safety tool that ensured none of us would be alone in our attempt to summit. There was not a lot of chatting going on; everyone seemed more aware of their movements and breathing. I was simply trying to breathe and keep my breathing calm and steady. I had no idea what a proper pace at altitude was; I just went as fast as I could.

Alicia Nelson, the youngest of our group, was my partner. A trainer at Malibu Fitness, she and I were closest in our fitness levels. Our pace was a little faster than the others who were behind us.

The trail was single-track and surrounded by beautiful trees, but my eyes focused on the ground, which was illuminated by my headlamp and the light from the headlamps around me. It was difficult, yet very doable. I tend to go faster in the dark, when my head is down, focused solely on whatever my headlamp is shining on. In this case, it was the dirt and rocky path under my feet, but looking down didn't always keep us on the trail.

After climbing above the tree line, Alicia and I got a bit lost and ended up on a steep, icy slope, having veered off the switchbacks that were mostly covered in snow. We didn't have crampons, which are like cleats for ice, or an ice axe, and there was nothing but a field of boulders to break our fall had either of us slipped. I was face-in toward the mountain, almost spreadeagle, literally holding on for dear life. My heart pounded with fear as sweat dripped down my shirt and, when I recognized the dire situation we were in, I thought, *I like my life. What am I doing here?*

A climber came by and kicked big steps into the side of the mountain for us to follow. That man, whom we didn't know, saved us and provided my first lesson in mountaineering—kick in good steps!

By the time the sun came up, Alicia and I were beyond sight of the rest of the group. Mount Whitney's sunrise was spectacular, as the route faces east most of the way up the main trail. I wasn't concerned about our friends behind us because everyone was strong and everyone had a buddy who would be with them the entire climb. I focused on the summit and getting to it—no matter what. During the almost eight-hour hike up the mountain, I designed houses in my head. I also replayed relationship issues and how to fix them, or not. Without my realizing it, my thoughts were occupied by all the things I would tell a therapist. I knew that those precious quiet moments allowed me to come up with good ideas and better ways to behave. Being outdoors was my therapy. The quieting of my mind in the rhythm of my steps was similar to meditation. Hiking was my meditation, my therapy, and eventually, my escape.

Fifty feet below the summit, I could see the little makeshift hut at the top. As I approached the building, I had an epiphany. I wanted more! Alicia and I were exuberant as we signed our names in the summit logbook next to the hut. I was happy, but I didn't feel proud of my accomplishment or take time to relish it. I wasn't appreciative of what I had just experienced. I only knew I wanted more! I was hooked. I wanted more of this physically demanding, personally empowering conquering of the unknown, and all the adventure that came with it.

Standing at the top of Mount Whitney, I asked, *What's next? What's higher?*

From the hut we walked over the boulders of the true summit, where the little round metal marker is attached to the rock. There we took photos to commemorate our success and sat down to enjoy our lunch. I had a bagel with cream cheese, ham, and white cheese. It was so great to eat real food. I also had a can of Coke. The bubbles felt so good in my mouth.

I was tired. We had just hiked for eight hours or so, mostly uphill, so I sprawled out on a boulder to take a short nap. After about an hour, I awoke with my head pounding, as if I had chugged an entire bottle of whiskey. I told Alicia I couldn't wait for the rest of the group. I had a horrid headache, and I knew that this was a sign of altitude sickness. The high altitude and low oxygen were getting to me. I slowly stood up. Feeling a bit dizzy, I put my pack back on and started toward the hut to catch the trail back down.

As we headed down the mountain, we spotted Tracy, Debbie, and Georgeanne, with her bright red hair. They'd made it! Each of us had a broad smile as we posed for a group photograph, but before we continued the trek down, we asked about the others in our group. They said everyone else was still on their way up. We left them to their experience of the summit and headed down the mountain.

About one hundred feet down the trail, we came upon Dale. She was pale, alone, and without the expensive new backpack she'd brought. A single water bottle hung from her wrist.

"Where is your pack?" I asked.
"I gave it to the Boy Scouts," she replied.

That seemed really odd because not only would you never give your pack away during a climb, but she also had had a brand-new, expensive water filter in that pack. She was the only one that had a filter, and I couldn't imagine her giving it away. The rest of us treated our water with iodine pills because we hadn't wanted to spend the money on a fancy water filter.

She could comprehend what we were saying, but her responses were not making sense. Always kind and smiling, my adventurous friend was not herself. Alicia offered her an ibuprofen. A minute later, I asked Dale if she had taken it. She was so disoriented that she couldn't recall if she had or hadn't. I handed her another one and watched as she put it into her mouth and swallowed. We pointed out the hut and told her how close she was to the summit and urged her to continue.

Even though Dale was all alone and missing all of her gear, it didn't occur to me—on that first climb—to stay with her and make her turn around with us. I didn't feel it was my place to tell her that. I was new to all of this and thought that reaching the summit was the only thing that mattered. I certainly wasn't going to deny her that experience. I didn't realize that it was okay to convince someone not to continue. I was so summit-crazed at that point that I would have been appalled at myself for even suggesting that she turn back. Alicia and I continued down, while Dale continued up to the summit and to our waiting friends.

For hours, Alicia and I maneuvered the never-ending switchbacks down the path. My feet ached, especially my toes, which were pressed hard against the front of my boots. Both Alicia and I spewed profanity every time we hit a rock or a root along the path, making my toes throb even more with debilitating pain. Finally, we arrived back at the portal.

To my surprise, Laureen, Laura, and Nan were waiting for us. They explained that they'd turned around hours before. Laureen didn't like the moonscape appearance of the mountain once you passed the tree line, and Nan had altitude sickness. Laura didn't want to continue up without them, so she too turned around.

They offered us a seat at the little café and presented us with boxes of chicken and steak. It was one of the most generous acts of kindness I had experienced. They weren't mad at themselves for not reaching the summit, and instead focused on what they could do for us. They asked if I'd go into the café to get drinks for everyone, which, despite my sore feet, I was happy to do. I looked up at the brightly lit menu behind the cashier and started to cry. I sobbed because of my friends' kindness, because of exhaustion, because I felt a sense of accomplishment, because…just because. I didn't know all the reasons for the tears, and I let them flow to the point where I was unable to order. Laura came in and ordered for us.

After devouring a delicious meal, Alicia and I went back to the Dow Villas Motel. I headed straight to my room, opened the phone book, and found a masseuse who would come to me. As I lay there on the table, I wondered how everyone else was doing. Were they back yet? I felt a slight twinge of guilt for lying there like a princess, getting a massage, and not being out there with my friends. When the masseuse left, I quietly hoped they had all arrived back safe, had had a good meal, and were nestled in a comfortable bed. Relaxed and exhausted, I fell into a deep sleep.

The next morning, I learned what had happened up there on the trail, and it wasn't good. Dale had arrived at the summit, but she was completely out of it. Tracy, Georgeanne, and Debbie saw her condition and tended to her as best they could before starting down the mountain. None of us had prepared to be out in the dark for two nights and, as they made their descent, all but one headlamp failed. These brave, caring women, on their very first climb, had to continue on in the dark, guided only by one dim light. When they arrived at the logs that you have to cross to avoid the little lakes and streams, Dale fell into the creek. Laying in the water, the only part of the event that she remembered was Tracy yelling at her, "Get up!"

Tracy is remarkably calm and no-nonsense, especially when presented with an obstacle or trauma. She instinctively seems to know what "mom voice" to use to reach the desired result. The mom of a special needs daughter, she's dealt with issues most of us never have to face, and she did it with a remarkable sense of grace. She was (and is) very determined and will deal with any obstacle she meets. In this case, the complication was Dale, and getting her back to a safe altitude as quickly as possible.

It took almost ten hours for the group to get down the mountain. They had returned to the Dow around eleven at night. At nine a.m. I knocked on Dale's motel room door. Her eyes were glassy and she wasn't feeling well. I was concerned about her, but proud of her for making the summit. I explained that I had to get home to my kids, which she acknowledged with a nod.

As I drove home, I felt guilty for having a massage and sleeping while my friends were out there struggling. I later learned that the other women took

Dale to the local emergency room shortly after I left. The advice the doctor gave was to get her back to sea level ASAP!

I learned so much from that trip. Kick into the mountain. A climb is not a race. Pace yourself. Prepare more. Most importantly, be there for others.

———

Today I have no problem telling someone to turn back if I think the situation isn't safe. I've had squabbles with people who didn't want to listen to that advice, only to have them blame me when they were stuck alone because of their stubborn desire to continue. It's a heavy burden not knowing where your friends are on a mountain or adventure. To have someone out there alone, needing help, is something I try to avoid. Someone thinking I would abandon them in the outdoors tears me apart. I learned from that first climb to never leave someone who was hurt or needed help. People die all the time because they don't stick to agreements, such as turnaround times, that are made pre-climb. Sometimes they push past all of their limits and have nothing left to get down.

I was, and am, so grateful that Dale had those three women with her. It took a while to forgive myself for the guilt I felt over leaving her. I simply didn't know better and was too summit-happy to suggest turning around. The mountain isn't going anywhere. If I don't feel well or am not getting a good vibe from the mountain, I simply turn around. It rarely happens, but I'm completely okay with it when it does.

Chapter 2

S omething had changed in my life, even though I was back at home and settled into my daily routine. I craved another experience where I could test myself on all levels. I began research for my next adventure and set my sights on Mount Kilimanjaro. It's one of the Seven Summits, so named because they comprise the highest mountains on each of the seven continents of the earth, which include Everest, Aconcagua, Denali, Kilimanjaro, Elbrus, Mount Vinson, and Carstensz Pyramid.

I openly stated to my family that I wanted to climb Kilimanjaro and, to my utter surprise, my husband was supportive of the idea. In fact, he invited an old friend from law school, along with the friend's girlfriend, to join us.

I knew this would be more of a challenge, but I felt it was doable, especially after I came across Alpine Ascents International, one of the largest climbing companies in North America, which specialized in the Seven Summits. They had excellent ratings and a high success rate. I figured if we were going to travel that far and pay that much, we should go with the best company so we could do this once and reach the summit, thus ensuring that we would never have to go back to try again.

Located in northeast Tanzania, Kilimanjaro is called "the Roof of Africa" because, at 19,341 feet, it's the tallest peak on that continent. This once-glacier-capped dormant volcano draws mountaineers from around the world who are willing to brave the high altitude, low temperatures, and sometimes-fierce winds. I knew it would be no small undertaking, and I knew that making it to the summit was not guaranteed. Some had even died trying. This trek would not be a one-day, turn-around trip like Mount Whitney.

I arranged for Alpine Ascents to act as our guides, and they would supply all food, tents, and porters for the trip. I felt mentally prepared for this climb and excited about it. I had summited 14,505 feet with no issues, and now I wanted to know what 19,341 feet felt like. An escalating inner challenge kept me wondering: would I summit?

My husband, who had more outdoor experience than me, knew the gear we needed. In addition, Alpine sent an extensive list, and we went shopping. We needed everything from sleeping bags, backpacks, headlamps, warm boots, really warm wool socks, and hand warmers to layers of clothing including Capilene tech shirts, fleece, and down jackets. That was all topped with a Gore-Tex parka. The final accoutrements were warm hats, gloves, and glacier glasses, which are designed to protect your eyes from the bright light in front of you, the glare bouncing off the ice below you, and all types of light that could reach your eyes from the side. It was an expensive shopping trip, but I felt that someone in our family would probably use the gear again. It didn't seem impractical at the time, but I remember wondering how much weight I would lose and how many calories I'd burn, and that I couldn't wait to wear my cute safari clothes on the trip we'd planned after the climb.

The day of our departure arrived. We spent the first two nights in London and then flew on to Kenya, where we would join the other climbers for the bus ride to Arusha. The road was pitted with huge craters, and every so often the driver would stop and pay a group of kids to fill the massive holes so we could continue on our way. The local kids had quite a racket going. Kenya felt disquieting. I don't know what it was, but I was uncomfortable and stayed close to my husband.

After a few days in Arusha, we left early for the three-hour drive to the Machame Gate. The Gate was the less-frequented beginning point that Alpine Ascents had selected as our starting point for the Kilimanjaro climb. Our climb would last six days and take us up the southern, more scenic route of the mountain.

The last part of the road to Machame Gate was unpaved, and our Toyota Land Cruiser got stuck in the mud. It wasn't going to budge, and if we wanted to stay on schedule, we were told we'd have to walk the remainder of the way to the Gate. Anxious to get this ascent going, I gathered my day pack and hopped out. A way up what barely passed as a road, I had to pee, and stepped on a pile of brush that I thought covered solid ground. As soon as I stepped forward, I realized it was a cliff! I managed to regain my balance and lean away from it. I made a mental note. Lesson one from Kilimanjaro: know where your feet are and know what you are stepping on at all times.

We reached the Gate and chose the porters who would carry our equipment. Our group of fourteen watched in amazement as the incredibly strong men strapped big, awkward, heavy duffle bags full of expensive gear onto their heads and strode toward our first camp. I was shocked when I saw that some of them wore flip-flops, and one had on bowling shoes, and then I realized that they were all carrying far too much weight. I wondered how long it would be before someone stepped in to bring about better working conditions.

Each climber carried a day pack that usually contained a rain jacket and pants, some snacks, camera, sunscreen, hats, gloves, and down jacket. Most everyone carried at least two Nalgene bottles of water. Nalgene bottles were preferred because they were tough and lightweight. I opted to carry only one bottle to keep my pack lighter, which meant I had to drink more liquids than most at breakfast, lunch, and dinner. Each pack weighed around ten to fifteen pounds depending on what was carried. The porters carried the rest of the equipment. I felt so grateful for those men, who hauled all our stuff up the mountain.

Following the porters, our group began walking uphill. An hour later, we were still walking uphill. The upness didn't seem to end. It was a steady, plodding ascent through a slight drizzle up the forest trail at the base of the mountain. This was certainly not the Marangu Route, the oldest and more established trail, sarcastically called the Coca-Cola Route because it was easier, with less terrain grade. Our trail, the Machame Route, was a difficult, muddy, consistent incline. The constant chorus of "Porters on the right" or "Porters on the left" announced our cue to step to the side to let them pass. The air filled with the smell of ganja and sweet, pungent sweat when the porters lumbered past us, moving steadily to our camp. Monkeys chattering in the trees around us seemed to be cheering for us as we climbed. They made me smile, even though we'd been warned that they'd happily steal our lunch if we weren't paying attention.

Exhausted and covered in mud, we reached our first campsite at 9,400 feet. At every camp there was a book that each climber had to sign. We had to list our name, occupation, nationality, passport number, and date of birth. I didn't mind the basics, but there was no way I was writing down my passport number for everyone to see. Our guide quietly suggested that any nine-digit number would do. Feeling relieved that I could control some private information, and a little playful, I listed my occupation one day as pole-dancer. Another day, I decided I was an astrophysicist.

The tents had already been set up and the duffle bags placed in a pile to the side. We collected our bags of gear and lugged them to our tent. I rolled out the inflatable pad that would go under my sleeping bag. I hoped that it would provide insulation from the cold ground and a cushion from the rocky terrain. I unpacked my duffle bag and was then asked by my husband to unpack his. It seemed that, since he had paid for the trip, I was expected to pack and unpack for him every night and morning. I was tired and hungry, but I complied without a word.

Once the bags' contents were neatly laid out, I changed from my trekking clothes to sweats and looked around the tent. In anticipation of what would unfold over the coming days, I smiled at the gear strewn about the little canvas enclosure. I grabbed my down jacket, stuffed my headlamp into my pocket, and headed to the dining tent. This had been an amazing day for me! The first leg of this adventure was complete.

Breakfast consisted of eggs, toast, fresh avocado, bacon, and porridge that I knew would help with hydration because of the water content. I topped it off with three cups of coffee and a lot of juice. I repacked our duffle bags and was ready to set out.

We continued ascending and crossed a little valley and a steep rocky ridge. The scenery seemed to change with every step toward the Shira Camp Kilimanjaro, our next overnight spot. Due to my fast-walking pace, I took the lead within our foursome. When I looked back and saw the scowl on my husband's face, I realized he was not happy with me in that position. I hung back a bit and let him pass, then continued onward and upward behind him. I subdued my frustration and turned my thoughts to our three children. I wondered what they were doing, and if they were behaving for their aunt, who had volunteered to watch over them so we could make this trek.

After several hours, we reached Shira Camp. The terrain was different. This was more like a desert at 12,500 feet, and probably the first camp where people might begin feeling the effects of altitude sickness. I felt fine. I obediently unpacked our duffle bags, inflated the pads to go under our sleeping bags, changed into warm fleece sweats, donned my big down jacket, and headed to the dining tent. The appetizers were popcorn or cheese and crackers before the main meal of chicken or beef, salad, rice, beans, and fresh vegetables. Dessert was either canned or fresh fruit and, if it happened to be someone's birthday, we had cake.

My husband was in a mood. And when I announced that I wanted to climb all Seven Summits, he rolled his eyes and ignored my declaration. I had irritated him again, but I wasn't about to let him take the joy out of my summit experience. He didn't like that I had passed him on the trail, and apparently, I'd said something that he wasn't happy with or that had embarrassed him. He completely ignored me during dinner and turned all of his attention to his law-school buddy and his girlfriend before he returned to our tent to sleep.

I sat outside our tent on the Shira Plateau and looked up at the stars and out over the stunning Kilimanjaro Valley below. Somehow, amid all the personal turmoil, I was able to be so present that I felt that all was right with the world. It's that rare feeling that there is no place you'd rather be or should be than right here, right now, in this moment. I had never felt that before, and I took it as a sign. And, just as with Mount Whitney, I wanted that feeling again.

The following morning, we continued up a ridge toward the Lava Tower, also called the Shark's Tooth, a remnant of the mountain's active volcanic days. The craggy rocky outcropping led us to the Barranco Camp, where we could see the Arrow Glacier on the side of the mountain.

The third, fourth, and fifth day sort of blended together. We hiked the incline and arrived at the camp, where I unpacked the duffle bags and organized what I removed from them, inflated the sleeping pads, and laid out the sleeping bags. Then I'd change clothes and go eat, return to the tent, sleep, and rise to start the morning process all over again. The best thing was the clean, fuzzy sleeping socks that I put on every night to keep my feet warm.

I was surprised at and shocked by the litter I saw along the trail. I watched a French-speaking man who was climbing with another group throw his candy wrapper on the ground. I was incensed. Who litters? Even worse, who goes to someone else's country and litters on their mountain? I picked up his wrapper and muttered "Asshole" under my breath.

On the night of the summit, our guide, Wally Berg, woke us at ten p.m. to give us time to gather our things, organize our gear for the summit, and have a small bite to eat before we began the climb. The first goal of the day was to reach Stella Point to experience the sunrise. For me, it was a very special day in the year before the new millennium.

It was really cold, and the stars in the sky made it look as if God had vomited stars—billions of sparkling orbs filled the heavens! We huddled together on a tarp and had coffee and some biscuits—a far cry from the large, warm breakfast served in a dining tent that is standard now. We stood up, grabbed our backpacks, which were pretty light as we were wearing all of our warm things, and started up the large rocky outcroppings on our way to the summit.

Our guide kept a really slow pace to help prevent climbers from getting sick. I was tired and freezing, and the slow, monotonous pace had me falling over sideways. I have walked fast since kindergarten, and this crawl of a pace was something new. It wasn't fast enough to warm myself and the rhythmic, slow steps almost put me to sleep. The monotony was broken only because we stopped every hour for a bite to eat and something to drink.

I was thrilled when we finally reached Stella Point, on the rim of the crater. Awaiting those first golden rays, we huddled together to stay warm and watched the morning sun color the sparse clouds as it rose over the African landscape. It was breathtaking, but I was ready to finish this trek.

We had only about an hour's hike left and, from that point onward, we were allowed to walk at our own pace to the final/true summit at Uhuru Peak. I looked around and thought about the four members of our group who weren't here to experience the moment. Three of the four had decided not to even attempt the climb. They weren't physically fit and recognized the potential problems. The other felt too sick and turned back. One of them had said, "I heard it was just a walk," only to discover that it is actually a formidable ascent. Technically, it is just a walk—a walk that takes you to an elevation of nineteen thousand feet on a steep mountainside. I couldn't imagine not putting in some training time and traveling all this way without even making an attempt to summit.

The ice fascinated me as we approached the summit. Sometimes it was up to my knees and sometimes up to my armpits. Despite the ice and the cold, I pressed on and, when we reached the ice-capped Uhuru Peak, it was like standing atop the world. I was at Africa's highest point, on the world's largest freestanding volcano! Uhuru was appropriately named, as it is the Swahili word for *freedom*. I had made it! And this experience, like Whitney, made me feel alive, empowered, and free.

Within hours of our return to California, we fell right back into typical routines. My husband left early for work while I got the children ready for their school day, puttered around the house, and relished my time with friends at the gym before collecting the children and delivering them to their after-school activities. I was still caught in my own destructive web of trying to be the perfect wife, holding my tongue when I wanted to speak up and purging to maintain an unhealthy weight but an acceptable presentation to the world.

We talked about climbing another mountain together and set our sights on the second-easiest of the Seven Summits, Mount Elbrus in Russia. I missed the high that came with the successful completion of an intense physical achievement. I had friends and acquaintances, but our adventures were limited to the gym or hikes through the local canyons. But, sometimes, life provides introductions that alter the path you think you've chosen.

A mutual friend introduced me to Dianne Burnett. Her two sons were the same ages as Johnny and Olivia. We became immediate friends and shared stories about our children, their projects, goals, and the typical parental concerns of the day. At the time, Dianne was married to Mark Burnett, an award-winning television producer and the executive producer of the successful television reality show *Eco-Challenge*. I told her about our recent trek up "Kili," a nickname for Kilimanjaro. Dianne was having a celebration for her son's birthday and invited us to the party. Not one for children's parties, my husband, after some discussion, reluctantly agreed to come along.

Introducing us, Dianne relayed to Mark that we had just climbed Kilimanjaro. With a smile and a rich British accent, Mark said, "You should try my race."

Without any hesitation, my husband and I looked at each other and blurted out, "Yes!" There was no discussion.

Mark doesn't kid around much, and I took his offer seriously. He might have thought that we wouldn't pursue his suggestion, and I'm certain he didn't know that what he said was the ultimate fantasy invitation to someone— me—who desperately wanted to participate in his race. In fact, I had wanted to join a team since I first watched *Eco-Challenge* on TV. I remember yelling at the competitors as they struggled through the contest: "Keep going. Stop being pussies!" Or "I wouldn't have stopped. Ever! I would have kept going." It was typical armchair quarterbacking with zero understanding of what these competitors were going through.

This was a dream come true and a game-changer for me, even though Mark cautioned us that he'd seen adventure racing cause separations and even divorce. That didn't curtail my enthusiasm. As far as I was concerned, I came away with quite the party favor—a quasi-invite to Mark's race.

The Eco-Challenge is an expedition-length adventure race and, realistically, the toughest race in the world. It's typically over three hundred miles through rough, rugged terrain. It's nonstop, twenty-four hours a day. GPS and other mapping devices are forbidden. Each team must navigate the course with only a map and a compass. All members of each four-person team do the entire race together and must finish together. There's always at least one member of the opposite sex on the team, and the disciplines of each race vary depending on the terrain. If any member becomes ill, injured, or totally exhausted and cannot continue, the team is disqualified. It is a race to see which team can face extreme stress and sheer exhaustion while problem-solving on the go, and still come in first.

We were serious about the prospect but needed a crash course in this type of competition. My experience level was so nonexistent that I didn't even know the difference between a mountain bike and a road bike. After several conversations with Mark, he connected us with two seasoned racers who had a lot of talent, but no money to race. We needed to learn everything about racing, especially about the many different disciplines. Financing the training and the race seemed an equitable exchange for our tutoring. An agreement was struck. My husband would financially front everything if Jason Middleton, our team captain, and Mike Trisler, a former Army Ranger, trained and prepared us in every way possible for Eco-Challenge Borneo 2000.

We had a year to get ready for the race, and the regimen would be intense. Fortunately, we were both physically fit, although my husband had a decidedly stronger base than me. He had played football and had done some backpacking and climbing while in college, ran almost every day, and had a weekly three-hour basketball game. Not one to lounge by the pool or on the beach, he never avoided any type of physical activity during a vacation. This particular challenge in Borneo included outrigger paddling, trekking, mountain biking, swimming, climbing, rappelling, etc. It was a huge physical undertaking, but we knew we could prepare for it. We didn't know how the tremendous mental strain and lack of sleep would affect us.

So we could better understand the subtleties of navigating the ocean, and to help establish the stamina we'd need for the race, we kayaked from Malibu to Marina del Rey. The repetitive paddling motion was broken only by brief breaks to hydrate or grab a quick snack. Then it was back to paddling, adjust course, and paddle more. I knew I was strong, but my tired muscles reminded me that I could be stronger.

Our first team-training race was the Corsica Raid, an exceptional adventure race that requires multiple disciplines to complete the difficult course. The Mediterranean island offered craggy mountains, dense forests, and a variety of aquatic experiences for a seasoned racer. It was a beautiful area with warm, friendly people and distinct topography. Our route included miles and miles of hiking—sometimes over high mountain passes—mountain biking, and climbing on a via ferrata, which employs cables, rungs, and ladders that a climber can secure themselves to in order to prevent catastrophic injury. The Corsica Raid provided us with the experience of canyoneering, which implements a range of techniques that includes hiking with ropes to explore the length of a canyon. We had to rappel down steep cliffs and, unfortunately, I rappelled down a sheer face too quickly, only for the canyon wall to disappear. I swung into a cave too fast and slammed my ankle into the rock wall. Despite the injury to my ankle, I was able to stay in the race for another day. I felt like a child reclaiming her childhood.

When we returned home, Johnny cried when he saw my bruised and bandaged body walk through the door. He said he didn't like to see me hurt and couldn't understand why I did this and why it was important to me. I knew it was difficult for an eight-year-old to understand. Sometimes I couldn't put it into words, either.

We took the kids with us to the north shore of Hawaii to pursue more intense training for the upcoming Borneo challenge. With the extreme physical activity, I rapidly began to lose weight, so much so that my teammates were horrified. Eating became a part of training. It was decided that I would have breakfast before anyone woke up and then again later, with the team. How ironic it seemed that I had spent all of those years trying not to gain an ounce and remain unrealistically thin, and now my goal was to gain weight.

Training and racing while raising three young children was brutal. We were all miserable. The kids didn't like the fact that their parents were perpetually training for various disciplines and not spending the amount of time with them that they'd become accustomed to. I hoped that at some point they'd understand that I had to do this.

My marriage was severely strained; when he wasn't training, he was working. My ankle had healed, and I was still pushing myself physically and purging to be the perfect Malibu wife, although I felt conflicted between my two goals. Would I be my husband's definition of the ideal wife, or would I be an adventure racer? Adding to the pressure, we were told that we, as a team, would be covered by the television show *48 Hours* as a means of promoting the challenge.

On a morning hike in the Santa Monica Mountains, walking briskly on dirt and small rocks on a hard-packed single-track trail, it finally hit me: I could either keep chasing the ideal thinness that gave me a sense of control, or I could gain weight and be a strong racer. It was a bit frightening when I realized I had to choose which path I was going to take. For the first time, I wanted something other than to be ninety-nine pounds. Adventure racing was the one thing that was more important to me than being a perfectly thin Malibu housewife.

I gave up purging and attacked adventure race training with a vengeance. The stronger I got physically through training, the stronger I got mentally. I stopped throwing up. I stopped restricting calories. Something clicked in my head that I needed those calories not only to live, but to be strong. The realization came to me that I wouldn't gain one hundred pounds by eating a normal lunch or dinner. I vowed to be strong, not skinny.

I knew my regime would continue to take a toll on my family, but I was willing to accept that. With that decision, my whole life changed. Everything I did was about training and being the strongest. I wanted to be a duplicate of the racer I had watched on television and most admired, Dominique Arduin of Team Nokia. She was like a machine, physically strong, and mentally unfazed and unaffected by pain. I wanted to be just like her.

Eco-Challenge Borneo was being held on the ocean and in Borneo's thick, leech-ridden jungle. Based in the town of Semporna, seventy-six teams paddled local *perahu* outrigger canoes to islands. Some teams had attached sails to help their crossing and some just paddled. We had a clever secret weapon—a kite that helped us reach the island first.

The next phase of the challenge put Mike and me on a ten-mile hike through some of the most treacherous jungle on the planet. It was thick and deep with undergrowth, spiked vines, and moist rotting foliage. My feet were always wet. The heat and humidity were awful, and the insects and leeches were perpetual pests. The weight we carried was a major consideration in dragging a pack through the jungle. I didn't bring insect repellent because bugs are usually not the worst of my problems, and weren't something I paid much attention to, even though other racers were covered in welts from bites and stings.

The absolute worst that the jungle offered me was the leeches. The little blood-sucking worms collected on us every time we were in the jungle. They literally dripped off the trees. They were so slimy that they easily slid through the mesh of our running shoes and worked their way under our pant legs or shirtsleeves. We were constantly stopping to pull them off each other. If they happened to get into an open wound, the pain they caused was excruciating. To me, leeches were the things that make up nightmares and the worst creatures I'd ever dealt with.

Mike, a former Army Ranger who called me "Token" because I was the sole female member of the team, was better prepared for this terrain than I was. Leeches or no leeches, I carried on, determined to do well on this leg of the adventure.

At one point along the jungle hike, I looked up and saw Dominique Arduin. She was a heroine to any adventure racer. I had watched her on other Eco-Challenges on television as she trudged on through the worst imaginable situations, no matter the environment, and never showed a hint of frustration or pain. She was a legend, and a woman I respected and strived to emulate because she seemed to detach from all emotional and physical reactions. When I saw her, I acted like a teenager coming face to face with their movie star or singing idol. She glanced in my direction and basically ignored me. On some deeper level, I understood that it wasn't personal; it was just who she was and, to be honest, we were in the middle of a jungle, racing against each other.

When we emerged from the jungle, we were in third place. The tangled green maze had put us back a bit.

Back in the canoes for another long paddling session, I hoped my feet would have time to dry out. That didn't happen. From the canoes we went to our mountain bikes for a sixty-mile ride. Our team was exhausted. Everything ached, but I tried to put that out of my mind. We hadn't slept much, only catching an hour or so whenever we could, but our spirits were high. We could still reach the finish line first.

The next leg of the competition took us back into the jungle. Everything was wet and the footing was slippery at best. The dense canopy of the trees prevented the sun from drying the forest floor. The sickening sweet smell of rotting vegetation permeated the air. We wandered around for hours, lost.

One night in the jungle, along the path, I saw a nun, kneeling in prayer as I made my way down the course. On some level I understood she was praying for me, for us. I blinked and she was gone. I wondered if it was one of the hallucinations I'd heard other racers speak of, or if she was a guide, a guardian angel looking out for us. It didn't matter to me in that moment; I was just pleased that she was there, offering her prayers. We made it out with blistered feet, but we'd had fallen way off our time. From the jungle we began a long river swim, followed by seventy-two miles of paddling a boat.

Our team entered the cold river water and started swimming downstream. It was going to be nice to be off our feet for the ten or so miles we needed to swim.

When we came to a big rapid, we had trained to go to the "V" shape, feet first. Mike and I were paired together, as were Jason and my husband. Everything was going fairly well, except for the extreme cold. Then we came up to the biggest rapid yet. Mike and I went over the rapid, feet first, and straight down into a hole. I have no idea how deep it was, but we were now under water and not coming back up. It was deeper than Mike's more-than-six-foot height.

Almost immediately, I was floating outside of my body, and I could see Mike to my physical body's left and the rope that was tied to our backpacks. The rope was tethered to him, so he could pull the packs while we had our arms free to swim. I saw the rope going across my body with the packs to my right. The force of the water held the two of us down. The rope held me back against a rock. I couldn't move, but I felt no need to struggle. I felt no fear, just amazement that, after everything I had been through in life, this was how I might die.

Not even a second after that thought was complete, we were forcefully regurgitated back up to the surface. Mike and I grabbed one of the boulders to our right. My fingertips tightly held on with everything I had until we pulled ourselves out of the swirling water. Ten feet farther down the river, swimming freely again, we looked at each other and started laughing. We had survived.

After our team came out of the water, a decision was made by the race director to have any team that had not yet entered the river to walk to the next checkpoint. I was told that when they were designing and testing the river portion of the course, it was the dry season and the water level had been low. But this was the rainy season. They halted the river swim, as the race directors felt it was too dangerous to continue.

We transitioned to a large, heavy boat, paddling in a strong current, and an even stronger rainstorm. Pushing myself harder and harder, I had a couple of epiphanies. The first was that I could divorce my husband and that I would survive it. That acknowledgement felt empowering and provided a momentary energy boost.

There was a competition rule that no one could be on the river after nightfall. We were being pelted by rain and realized evening was approaching. We pulled the cumbersome four-person wooden boat out of the water and onto a small beach, then tipped it onto its side and all of us crawled under it. Mike pulled back the wet bark from some twigs and made a small fire. Sitting under that canoe, I was struck by the second epiphany of the day: All I needed in life were my children, a couple of friends, shelter, warmth, and food. Anything beyond that was gravy.

We continued the journey at sunrise the following morning and paddled for most of the day and into the night again. My feet still weren't dry. I know I was functioning on very little sleep, moody, and starving. In fact, I was so hungry that, while portaging the boat over some boulders, I spotted a discarded, wet Wheat Thin on a rock, scraped it off, and ate it.

I was feeling empowered by what I had survived so far. When we pulled the canoe out of the water for the last time, to transition to another discipline, I turned to face a camera. I don't know where it came from, but I announced to the television camera recording our movements that my marriage was over. I meant it, and in that moment, I didn't care who knew it.

Our physical condition had deteriorated beyond anything we expected, although mentally we wanted to keep going. We hiked for a few more miles, but as a team, we were at a crossroads. Mike, a stuntman, had signed on to do a movie that he had to be back in the States to start. He'd come to Borneo knowing he had only three days to race, and if we weren't going to win, he was not going to stay and finish. Our feet were trashed, and I could barely walk. Of all the things that Jason and Mike had taught us during our intense pre-race training, there was only one thing they'd never mentioned, and that was foot care. If we had only had some Vaseline, all those blisters might have been avoided.

While the cameras rolled, we had a lengthy conversation about quitting. Mike and Jason wanted us to say we were quitting, instead of Mike taking that responsibility by saying he was quitting to go do a movie. We didn't want to cave in and be the reason for quitting, but after examining the wounds on our feet, we decided to seek the advice of the race doctors. They determined that I had the beginnings of jungle rot. Our race was over, and the next morning, I was carried onto a plane. I was disappointed, mostly in myself, but there was no way I could continue without doing irreparable damage to my body.

I was moved to a hospital in Kota Kinabalu. My feet had to be debrided, and the medical team said I would probably require surgery to remove badly infected skin on my feet, butt, and arm. They explained that the dead skin had to be removed so the wounds could heal properly. It's a painful procedure, and it can take weeks for the wounds to thoroughly mend. At one point while in the hospital, I had to pee so badly that I crawled on my hands and knees to the toilet. I hoped that that was as low in life as I would ever go.

When I finally saw my horribly matted hair in the bathroom mirror, I cut off inches, knowing I didn't have the energy to try to untangle it. There was no vanity or ego left. I didn't care if I had to crawl because my feet hurt too much to stand and walk, or if my hair looked like it had been coifed with a lawn mower. There was nothing left.

On the bright side, my hospital roommate was none other than Dominique. When I arrived at our shared room, she came over and sat on the side of my bed. I felt so honored. She was speaking to me! She explained that her life had been difficult. She told me that her husband and son had died in an automobile accident. I realized that that was why she could race like she did—she had nothing left to lose. Implacable and independent, with numerous achievements under her belt, she was planning her next event: a solo ski trip to the North Pole.

My injuries were improving, but the doctor had to change the gauze bandages that covered my raw feet before he would release me. His hospital was now filled with racers and he needed the room. He told me to hold onto the side

of the gurney so he could remove the bandages from my feet. He had to rip
the gauze from my skin, which had grown over the bandages as the wounds
healed. He yanked and I screamed the F-word. It was agonizing. As he
reapplied fresh gauze to my tender feet, he looked me in the eye and asked
me why we do such a sport. I looked back at him blankly. I didn't have a
good answer.

We returned home, and somehow moved past the Eco-Challenge Borneo
experience and got back into the regular routine of life with three young
children. Our marriage had always been difficult, and it remained so, with the
usual ups and downs. Following a routine of work, school, and activities made
it easier to ignore feelings and problems by being too busy to address them.
Despite my first epiphany, it was easier for me to keep walking on eggshells,
keep up appearances, and not file for divorce.

Eco-Challenge Borneo was seen by most of our friends, and my proclamation
that my marriage was over took everyone by surprise. I regret that I said that
on television. I knew it was hurtful, and I'm sure it was one of the many nails
in the coffin of our marriage. The race had tested both of us, and we didn't
look good on the program. The extreme mental and emotional pressure,
along with the harsh environment and minimal conditions for survival,
were beyond our worst expectations. The experiences in Borneo had further
shredded our relationship. We tried counseling, going from one therapist
to another. Most of them told me I should leave, but I tried to repress my
dissatisfaction with life and hold on to an appearance of normalcy.

In addition to feeling strong when I raced, I also felt that I was actually good at
something. Too often I felt as though I wasn't a good enough wife or mother,
which had been reinforced by my husband numerous times. To get validation
from others that I was good at something helped me find a positive light in
myself. Who would want to give that recognition up? The support from others
and the high that one gets from adventure racing were not things I wanted
to abandon.

Mike and Jason taught me so much about multiple-disciplined sports and, as much as I loved racing, nothing was more important to me than my kids. Yet, the internal need and drive to continue racing was now a part of me, too, and something that I felt had to continue. I carefully weighed my family commitments and my desire to race and decided I could manage two races a year and still be a hands-on mom for my kids if I only trained while my kids were in school.

My marital relationship was becoming a perpetual irritant. We started negotiating the continuation of our marriage, trying to find things that could potentially keep us together. I wanted to do two big races a year. I'd be gone for two weeks or less, twice a year. That was approximately the amount of time that my husband spent on boys' trips or nights out with his friends. During the negotiations to stay married, he decided he wanted me to do zero races. With that, we were no longer negotiating a marriage; we were bargaining a separation. That became very apparent when he demanded I sign a post-nuptial agreement giving up any rights to his social security, collect no alimony, and a bunch of other mean-spirited things that were designed to punish me.

I refused to be deterred and pursued my passion to race. I felt a sense of independence, even though my confidence was shaken by the horrible ending to the Borneo challenge. I was determined to continue training, which made him uncomfortable. He began to realize this was not a passing fancy or a one-time thing for me, and he gave me an ultimatum: quit racing or get a divorce.

I didn't want to go back to being an anorexic housewife. I didn't want to go back to being that weak woman I was before adventure sports came into my life. I thought we could compromise, but nothing was acceptable to him.

Finally, one morning, right after we had sex, he casually said while stepping into the shower, "By the way, I'm divorcing you."

"Great," I replied sarcastically, trying to mask my shock and humiliation.

Divorce it would be. I was hurt and angry, but at that point I didn't care what happened next. I only knew that I didn't need to live in a mansion or drive fancy cars. I wasn't into the latest fashions or designer labels. I was no longer willing to be controlled. I had finally begun to find out who Dianette really was, and I wasn't about to relinquish that discovery to anyone else.

Chapter 3

I signed up for my first ultra solo race, the Alaska Iditasport. This extreme race takes place in the dead of winter and begins at Knik, the birthplace of the Iditarod Trail Sled Dog Race and follows the famed Iditarod Trail. There are three lengths to the race: 130 miles, 350 miles, and the full 1,100 miles to Nome. Each racer can choose to compete on skis, on a bike, or on foot. I decided to run the course. I was in a bad headspace after Eco Borneo and only wanted to prove to myself that I could still function as an athlete, so I chose the shortest of the three distances. I also didn't want to be away from the kids for too long a time.

The course winds its way to Susitna River and up the Yentna River to the Yentna Station checkpoint (Mile 60). The trail continues up the Yentna River another thirty miles to the Skwentna Roadhouse checkpoint (Mile 90). Leaving the river system, the course then heads overland into the Shell Hills to the Shell Lake Lodge optional checkpoint (Mile 105). There the trail begins to climb into the foothills of the Alaska Range, coming to the Winter Lake checkpoint at Finger Lake (Mile 130). That was the end of the short course.

The first morning, the race director asked me what a Malibu housewife was doing in Alaska running his race. He was genuinely curious and seemed unconvinced that I belonged there. I smiled, knowing that, at this point in my life, his comment would act as motivation.

The conditions were biting cold. The average high temperature was twenty-two degrees Fahrenheit and the low was six degrees. In mid-January, there are only about six hours of sunlight, and much of the race is run in the dark.

I carried everything on my back. I realized my best course was slow and steady across this vast frozen wilderness. It was exhausting, and yet exhilarating. The first couple of days were heaven. I was alone, responsible solely for myself, and regaining my strength and confidence with every step.

Brutal winds and a harsh winter storm blanketed the course, making it even more difficult to continue. I was exhausted, but pushed on with little more than an hour of sleep until I knew couldn't go any farther. Right on the trail,

I pulled out my sleeping bag, stepped into it and then into my bivy sack, and then I just fell over on my side. I knew that if I froze on this tundra in a blizzard, at least my body would be found because I was on the trail. Several times people came up and shook me to see if I was alive. I mumbled and they continued on while I settled back into a frosty sleep.

Renewed by a minimal amount of sleep, I pursued my goal. At one point I was in a small hut where several racers—runners, fat-tire mountain bikers, and cross-country skiers—had gathered. They were ready to call it quits, and I understood why. What should have been a two-to-three-day race was turning into five tortuous days.

I pulled out my satellite phone and stared at it. Ella was in class and I knew her school wouldn't put me through to her. Olivia was too young to reach out to and I didn't want to upset her, so I called Johnny from the warm hut. As I dialed, I remembered the tears in his eyes when he saw the physical shape I was in after Eco Borneo. I needed to hear a voice from home. He was in class at Point Dume Marine Science School and, as would become the norm with the wonderful ladies in the front office, my call was put through to his classroom. I told him what was going on and that I was thinking of quitting because, if I stayed and finished the course, I would be a couple of days late coming home.

"Don't quit, Mom," was his staunch reply. It was almost a demand.

Those words were all I needed to hear. I ended up placing second out of the eight female runners in the 130-mile division. The six other women had quit. I didn't care what place I came in. I had finished the race, my personal challenge, and I was on a high. My confidence was back and I was ready to race again.

I focused on healthier, more balanced ways of training. I didn't need to intensely train six to eight hours a day, six or seven days a week. I had a strong base, but I needed my physical training to harmonize with my home life. Fortunately, I had a like-minded friend, Lynn Jacob, who knew great trails and was an awesome mountain biker. She was a gift at this time in my life. We would drop the kids off at school and then go ride our mountain bikes or hike until it was time to pick them up. Her son, Trevor, became best friends with Johnny. It was such fun being around the two boys. They were two peas in a pod, with moms to match. Lynn pushed me to train harder, smarter, and to not give up on my goals or myself. She understood my need to continue racing.

I felt renewed, and was asked to race Expedition BVI 2001, a five-day adventure race in the British Virgin Islands. I looked forward to the fact that there were no swamps or freezing temperatures to contend with, and that it was a five-to-six-day multi-disciplined course that included kayaking, biking, hiking, rappelling, and swimming.

I was racing with Team Challenged Athletes Foundation. Our challenged athlete, Willie Stewart, lost his arm in a construction accident and since then has competed in endurance and extreme sports contests, including finishing the Ironman on four occasions. He'd won a Paralympics medal for cross-country skiing and spent much of his time mentoring adaptive athletes. He was an inspiration to all he met. The camaraderie and demanding challenges only fueled my desire to continue adventure racing. We crossed the finish line, and I immediately caught a plane back to California.

It was good to get home and right back into the kids' routines. Ella was as studious as ever. She'd always been intellectually curious with a healthy desire to succeed at all she attempted. Olivia, the youngest, stayed close to me, a true mommy's girl. Johnny and his friend Trevor spent their spare time riding motorized dirt bikes. When they weren't zipping around on their dirt bikes or skateboards, they were at their friend Parker's house building ramps, berms, and jumps, or testing the half-pipe sitting in the driveway of Parker's home. Johnny was showing his desire to experiment with speed in almost everything he did, including building a concrete track that served as a skateboard luge.

I was receptive to letting my children try anything once, but I had one very explicit rule for them. They could only have two different activities or lessons per week, and if they signed up for something, they weren't allowed to quit. They had to finish what they signed up for, no matter if it was a sport or an educational class.

Due to my mom's long work hours as a nurse, my brother and I had enrolled in whatever sports and activities the local park was putting on. It was the '70s, and we pretty much had the run of the neighborhood. The only rule was that we had to be home when the streetlights came on. I remember sitting on the curb, being bored, if there were no friends available to play. In second or third grade, my mom's new husband appeared. She conveniently forgot to tell my brother and me that she had married. We heard that news from a kid down the street. My brother and I stayed away from the house every possible minute. We despised him.

As a racer, I began to examine what compelled my commitment to the sport. There are many competitors who say adventure racing is addictive. It's difficult to examine what addictive means when it comes to racing. Is it the release of endorphins through extreme physical activity? Is it the sense of accomplishment? Is it the self-challenge?

Everyone is different, and everyone races for personal reasons. The majority of individuals seem to be extremely disciplined, motivated, and definitely physically capable. They seem to be naturally equipped with a mental toughness, a competitive nature, intense focus, positive attitudes, and an ability to work with others. Some may be driven by the adrenaline rush, some by the self-challenge, and others by the need to excel at something unique.

I ask myself why I race every time I'm hungry, sleepless, or injured during a race. And after every race, I promise my kids I won't do it again. They've come to accept that I probably won't quit until my body gives out. It's an odd blessing but, because I'm an adventure athlete, the kids and I have had some wonderful experiences that we might not have had otherwise. Thankfully, they're very forgiving, and seem to understand that every race, every challenge is a means of self-discovery and empowerment. No matter what is thrown in my way, I will do my best to overcome it. To me, a racecourse is just another place to prove that to myself, but I often question the other things that I find compelling about racing. Is it because I love the camaraderie that comes with being fully dependent on three other people whom I trust with my life? Is it the silence of walking through the night in a remote place? Is it being mentally flexible enough to face all of the obstacles?

Flexibility is the complete opposite of my home life, where I am a control freak. I need my home and surroundings to be perfectly organized. I function well when my home is immaculate and things I can control surround me. There is zero control on a racecourse, except for your own mental toughness. Physically, when I'm exhausted and just want a warm bed and a large meal, my brain kicks in to tell me to, *Keep going, Mamacita! You've got this.* I definitely love the challenge of being on the start line not knowing if I will last one hour or eight days. That's part of the adventure of the unknown.

For almost all of us, at some point, we discuss seeking professional help for continuously wanting to race, searching for a rationale behind why we do this insane sport. That conversation inevitably ends with, "What are you signed up for next?"

––––––––––

The Discovery Channel World Championship Adventure Race was next on my docket. Forty-one teams from around the world had signed up, and I would be racing with Team Cure Parkinson's. The start point was scenic St. Moritz, Switzerland, at the end of August. This was billed as everything an adventure race should be. The course was 261 miles, and the disciplines included hiking, mountain biking, canyoneering, rafting, and climbing.

The six-day race began on a beautiful sunny day, at an elevation of over ten thousand feet, with a run down the Piz Corvatsch glacier. The views of the Alps and the valleys were spectacular, but no one took time to enjoy them. We were racing, and taking in the beauty of nature scenes wasn't on the itinerary.

Mapping out the course, we knew it would be arduous, but we'd heard that several teams had dropped out on the first day, which is unusual for such an experienced group of racers. Altitude sickness and hypothermia took some out; others left because of injuries. The first thirty-five miles was literally up and down. Every major descent was followed by a grueling ascent. The course was full of climbs and declinations that were achieved via a lot of hiking and biking, which we felt prepared to tackle.

On the second day, the weather grew inclement. Rain and snow hampered the racers who had reached the Viamala Gorge. The gorge's name literally translates to "bad route," and for a few of the racers, it lived up to its moniker.

The course had been planned in such a way that the racers would reach the gorge about sunup. Some teams had beaten the expected time and arrived at this ancient canyon in the dark hours before dawn. Already cold and physically wasted, they wiggled into their wetsuits, strapped on their life preservers, and rappelled seventy meters off a bridge to the river below. The rules said there was no swimming at night, and mandated that no one enter the water until six in the morning, at which time they could jump into the icy, glacier-fed river to begin a two-mile swim. Those who rappelled off the bridge in the dark and entered the cold water had to swim to a beach below the bridge and freeze for the night.

Harald Zundel, our team navigator and a former Navy SEAL, had determined it was best to stop and sleep before reaching the bridge. We'd be rested by six in the morning, when we could see what was waiting for us below.

We never made it to the bridge, but later learned that a member of the British team, Carolyn Jones, a former British National Rowing Championship gold medalist, had nearly drowned. She'd gotten caught in a furious current and her head, encased in a helmet, was jammed between two rocks under the surface. About twenty minutes passed before they got her out. They performed CPR and eventually airlifted her out to a hospital, where she was comatose.

Danger is always out there, whether it's in an adventure challenge or life. When you're racing, you can't stop to think *that might have been me.* If you do, fear takes over, and your overcaution could end up being as deadly as an accident. I try to stay focused on the next leg of the course, the next challenge, and not get caught up in what-if mind games.

Harald made another call during this race that saved our entire team. We were lost on the side of a cliff. According to our map, the village was right below us. It was; hundreds of feet straight down the cliff. It was the middle of the night, and we couldn't see the sheer ledge we were wandering around on. A producer for the TV show said they had watched us from the village below, our headlamps reflecting pinpoints of light on the mountainside. He later told me that they were sure one of us was going to fall off the cliff that night, and that several had stayed awake to keep vigil over our team precariously positioned on the mountain.

We could barely see a few feet in front of us when Harald made the usually unpopular decision to stop until we had daylight and could better assess our situation. He didn't feel right about something. Thank God he did that.

When dawn broke and we could see, we began to climb down the hillside a bit farther. Certain the trail was right below us, we were horrified to see just how close we had come to the edge. It was so steep that, while working our way back up the hillside, a teammate offered to tie himself to me to help me feel safer. I agreed for a short time. Then I realized that, if he fell, he'd take me down the hill with him, and if I fell, I would take him down with me. I quickly untied from him, took my gloves off, and dug my fingers into the ground as we climbed back up. As we slowly moved back up the hill to the trail, I made a mental promise to my kids: if I made it, I would never climb Mount Everest. I had also promised that I would never race again.

I thought about that specific promise I'd made three years earlier in Switzerland as I signed up to climb Mount Everest. A teammate once told me that God knows people make those types of promises under duress, and therefore they don't count. That rationalization worked for me.

A month later I was in New Zealand, participating in the almost two-hundred-mile-long Eco-Challenge across the country's Southern Alps. Seventy-five international teams signed up to test their skill and endurance. My husband was racing, too, but we were on separate teams. He captained his team and I was the captain of Team Cure Parkinson's/Gramicci. We mutually agreed to pull the children out of school so they could travel with us. We both felt that, whenever possible, it was important for them to experience the world, rather than only learn about it from a book. We brought a babysitter from Malibu to stay with the kids while we were on the course racing. I had only one rule for the babysitter and the kids: they could do whatever activity they wanted to do, except anything related to flying.

The Eco-Challenge races were Mark Burnett's babies. He had gained the respect of all the racers because he was always right there with them and for them. He cared about his racers, yet he realized that, as a race director, if the course wasn't putting the competitor at the edge of death or a total mental collapse, the racers weren't having fun and the audience wasn't either. But because of Carolyn's near-fatal accident during the Discovery Channel World Championships in Switzerland, Mark decided to dumb down the course. New Zealand was a boring race for the participants. As the teams easily finished the race, they told Mark that it was the worst race ever. We were all used to the extremes of adventure racing, but this course we could have done in our sleep. Mark took the criticism to heart and decided that the next one would be so difficult that only one team should finish. He was not kidding.

After my team crossed the finish line, when I was putting my gear away, a man walked up to me and asked for my brand-new tent. "What?" I asked in amazement.

"Your daughter said if I gave all the kids a ride in the helicopter that you would give me your tent when you were done racing," he replied with a smile of expectation.

Leave it to Ella, at the age of eleven, to score helicopter rides for everyone. I had to think and talk fast to avoid relinquishing my tent to the pilot. As

I walked away, I wondered if Mark knew that was happening in his Eco-Challenge helicopter.

My instructions had been specific. There was to be no activity related to flying. However, the stories and pictures of them paragliding and flying in a helicopter apparently didn't count as flying. Johnny had his first taste of flying while I was racing. In the photograph from his first paragliding flight, his face is up, and his arms are outstretched. He loved every second of that experience.

We had a few days left in New Zealand before we were scheduled to fly home, so we took the kids to the Kawarau River, home of the first commercial bungee jump. Our oldest and, at that time, the most intellectual, Ella, begged her dad and me to let her jump. After saying yes, she decided that she didn't want to do it alone, so she begged me to do it with her. I was still tired from the race and my defenses were low, so I agreed. Johnny, who had paraglided days earlier, was deathly afraid of heights and refused. I smiled at the contradiction and thought of the first time his fear of heights became apparent. He refused to look over the edge at the Hoover Dam, screaming as I picked him up to show him what it looked like. Johnny and Olivia watched while Ella and I made an exhilarating jump from the Kawarau Bridge.

My next race was the Raid Gauloises in Vietnam. The course was over six hundred miles long and was being touted as the longest raid ever. It went from the mountains in the east to the sea, and had fifty-two checkpoints and three assistance points. Each team was required to rest for three hours at the assistance points. There were no dark zones, which meant we'd be racing at night—even in water—as well as during the day.

That was my first time racing as a member of Team Stray Dogs. Legendary endurance athlete Marshall Ulrich was the team captain. The rest of the team included Adrian Crane, one of the world's best navigators, in my opinion; Chris Daugherty, a humble Navy SEAL; and uber long-distance runner Charlie Engle. Chris dropped out early. His feet were so raw they looked like hamburger. His departure meant we couldn't officially finish the race, so Marshall, who understandably didn't want to waste his time crossing the finish line unofficially, also left. That left Charlie, Adrian, the two crew members, Yee-Fung Wong and Nico Minerva, and me to finish what we had started.

The start point was a small village near the border with China called Bac Ha. The first part of the course took us through miles of dense vegetation covering steep mountains, then a downhill bike course that was followed by a rappel down a waterfall and into canoes. The compulsory three-hour rest at the assistance point was welcomed, but at the end of the time block we were back on our bikes, then navigating what felt like an impenetrable jungle to native bamboo rafts that were about twenty feet long.

It was an exhausting trek that took a toll on each of us. At one point, I fell asleep while riding a bike and sailed right over the handlebars, landing vertically headfirst. Toward the end of the race, I had become so dehydrated that I required two bags of IV fluids just to stand up. I was so thirsty when we reached one of our checkpoints that I couldn't even swallow the water that was offered to me. Because of my condition, the doctors weren't going to allow me to continue. After the IVs, I struggled to walk back to the team to tell them the bad news. Our crewmember grinned and shook her head. She pulled lipstick out of her bag, applied some to my lips and cheeks, put sunglasses on me and walked me back to the doctor to show him how much I had improved.

The doctors, surprised by the sudden improvement in my appearance, were happy that the IVs had worked and agreed to let us continue. My incredible team managed to help me into the canoe, which was already loaded with our bikes, and let me sleep as they paddled across the lake. When we reached the other side, the IV fluids had taken effect and I was good to go.

Vietnam was beautiful and it was frightening. We were always being followed. It seemed like everyone, including the Chinese, knew exactly where we were at all times. During a mountain bike section of the course, Charlie, Adrian, and I were pedaling our way through thick mud when we came to a fork in the road. According to the map, we needed to go to the right. As we made

that turn, Chinese police or military guards of some sort stopped us. Charlie
tried to explain that we needed to go that way. The discussion grew louder and
more animated. Charlie pointed to the map, and they shook their heads and
gestured that that was not possible. They went back and forth in two different
languages, neither one understanding the other. It was obvious that neither
side wanted to budge. I bent over my bike, closed my eyes, and tried to catch
a few minutes of sleep while they all argued. Finally, Adrian, the calm voice of
reason said, "Charlie, we have to go left. They have guns…"

I sat up, chuckling. That was the funniest thing I'd heard in a while, mostly
because it was frighteningly true.

The poverty of the country was heartbreaking, but the people were
remarkable. During a pounding rainstorm, we spotted a small house with a
covered porch. We didn't know if we'd be met by a caring villager or shot as
trespassers, but we needed a break from the rain. We parked our mountain
bikes under the eaves of the old house and huddled together to stay warm.
The night was pitch-black, except when the lightning would illuminate the
entire valley. It was breath-taking. We had just settled in when the front
door opened. I thought we would be thrown off this man's property. We
were strangers crashing on someone's porch in the middle of the night! To
the contrary, the older man motioned for us to come in. He offered us tea
and then pointed for us to lie on the dirt floor by the warm fire. I could hear
a small child with a horrible cough in a back room, and I wished I could do
something to help her. A couple of hours later when we woke up, he was still
there watching over us. We got up to leave and tried to give him money. He
refused. Not a word of English was spoken, and yet, that man's kindness stays
with me all these years later.

The jungle was so thick you couldn't see what was right next to you. If we got
off course, locals would pop out of the jungle to point us in the right direction.
We later learned that there were booby traps left over from the Vietnam War
and they were helping us avoid them by keeping us on track.

We were searching for a small opening in the thick overgrowth that would take us into a cave that would eventually lead us through a mountain. A young girl watched as we tried to decipher the map. She motioned for us to follow her and, after a brief debate about her knowledge of the racecourse, we did. She took us right to the small cave opening. I didn't think an adult could fit into such a small opening. Charlie went in first to see if he would fit. When he sounded the all-clear, we each shimmied into the hole. The cave wasn't too difficult to navigate, and we emerged on the other side of the mountain. I'll always appreciate the help we received from the people of Vietnam. They showed us deep acts of kindness that came from the heart. This type of experience happens to adventure racers over and over again, all over the world. It's one of the wonderful experiences that make it so important to me.

We crossed the finish line a couple of days later. And, as if the harshness of that race weren't enough, the bus we were traveling in after the race sideswiped a truck parked along the side of the road. The bus driver swerved away from the truck and ended up driving down the wrong side of the road into oncoming traffic. The driver found an opening and got us back on the right side of the road before pulling over. We climbed out of the now wide-open front window to wait for another bus to pick us up. I thought about the irony of the situation. I had just finished a grueling race that could have killed me at any time, and I nearly got killed in a bus accident on my way to the hotel.

Chapter 4

Johnny, climbing in the Tetons in Jackson Hole, Wyoming

A race director walks a fine line between making certain the competitors have the time of their lives and not killing them. Mark Burnett attracted the most amazing athletes from all around the world to the challenges, knowing that they yearned for more adventure and bigger obstacles to confront. Races needed to constantly evolve. The teams were comprised of men and women who endured days filled with suffering and adversity. Racers thrived on the unknown and on conquering whatever it presented. Even though he had intended to keep the competitors safe, he understood the disappointment some teams expressed after the relatively uncomplicated New Zealand course.

Mark also had to satisfy the viewers who would tune in to the challenges. It may seem to be a bizarre business model, but it had been successful. Mark was a master of bringing an enthusiastic television audience to watch the drama and trauma that world-class racers constantly faced in his contests.

He determined that Eco-Challenge Fiji 2002 would be different. It would be the world's toughest challenge yet. He had help with the design of the racecourse and all of the other details from Kevin Hodder, a very intelligent man who looks as though he's perpetually twelve. The design team also included Scott Flavelle, the statuesque Lisa Hennessy, and the always fun Tricia Middleton, among many others, but Mark set the tone. He was so resolved to make this a difficult course that he offered to return money to participants who decided they didn't want to compete prior to the start date. The specifics of the course would be kept under wraps, and no particulars were to be shared until the first day of the race. The only thing we knew was that the race was across the main Fijian island, Viti Levu, and traversed the highlands to the western coast and offshore islands.

Eighty-one teams signed up for the three-hundred-mile, ten-day odyssey. People from various career paths made up the mixed-gender teams and represented Argentina, Australia, Bermuda, Brazil, Canada, Chile, Costa Rica, Fiji, Finland, France, Guam, Hong Kong, Ireland, Japan, Mexico, the Netherlands, New Zealand, Norway, Panama, Singapore, South Africa, United Kingdom, Venezuela, and the United States. The rules remained the same. If one team member quit, for whatever reason, the entire team was disqualified.

Eleven months had passed since New Zealand, and I was looking forward to Fiji. Ella and Johnny were very busy with their friends, activities, and school. They were used to us leaving for Eco-Challenge races, as this was the third year we had done it. Life with three kids was crazy busy, and racing was just a part of the circus.

Johnny used to beg me to allow him to race. My son could be very persuasive, and in order to avoid a debate, I started blaming Mark and told Johnny, "It's against the law for you to race until you are eighteen," or "Talk to Mark about the rules." I knew that, as soon as he was old enough, he would race and I looked forward to racing with him.

As with the race in Vietnam, I was once again racing with Team Stray Dogs, whose other members included veteran Eco-Challenge racers Marshall Ulrich, Charlie Engle, and Mark Macy. Adrien Crane had a prior commitment to another team. We had some difficulty getting sponsors but picked up a few gear makers here and there. Money can be hard to find for racers, especially those who aren't involved with the sport on a full-time basis.

Around eleven at night, we were driven to our starting point, where we would sleep under the cold blanket of a drizzly night. A mixture of excitement, anxiety, and conviction welled inside me as I stepped off the bus into the grassy field. We would begin the journey that awaited us at dawn. The next morning, we raced down the slight incline to a river where we jumped into cold water for a bit of a hike and swim. That's when I found out that, as adept as he was in so many disciplines, Marshall couldn't really swim. Secretly, I thought that was really funny, because I had never shared with my teammates that I was afraid of heights. I realized we all have our Achilles heel to deal with on these expeditions. The great thing about adventure racing is that you don't have to be an expert at any one thing. It's far more important to be good at everything. You can have an expert mountain biker on the team, but if they

can't navigate a river, the team could easily be disqualified and forced out
of the race.

One team was out of the competition shortly after the start. A woman fell in
the somewhat shallow river and, exactly where her knee hit the bottom, there
was an eel. Needless to say, it bit her, and she went into anaphylactic shock.
Her team was out. An entire year of training and a large sum of money was
spent to be here, and it was over in mere hours. Events like that are completely
out of one's control, and it's one of the things that make crossing a finish line
that much sweeter. In adventure, you just never know.

One night, we faced navigating huge boulders protruding precariously in the
swift current of the river. We didn't think we were on the right course because
it was extremely treacherous. We couldn't imagine that Mark and his design
team would put us in that much danger, so we agreed to stop and wait for
daylight before continuing through that maze of rock and water. I was soaking
wet and had become hypothermic, shivering uncontrollably, and announced
to my teammates that I was dying. Even though I was freezing, I began to
take off all of my clothes. I heard one of them say, "Oh no!" When you're
hypothermic, your mind and body do not function as they should. They
managed to keep my clothes on me. Marshall then pulled a fleece sweatshirt
out of his pack and put it on me. I wondered who in the world would bring
a fleece to what I thought would be a hot and steamy jungle. Thankfully,
Marshall did, and it kept us in the race. My teammates huddled next to me,
trying to keep me warm. I was so out of it that I remember seeing a spider
crawling on the rocks above my head and saying to it, "You deserve to be
warm, too, little guy." We slept for a few hours in a dog pile and then, as dawn
broke, began to maneuver through the boulder field.

The course was almost impossible. The length of the course, the tangled
morass that covered the jungle terrain, the mud that was so thick we couldn't
ride our mountain bikes. We'd drag the bikes a few feet and then lift them
over our heads to throw it to the ground in hopes of getting the muck off
of them. We even tried carrying them on our backs. The mud clung to
everything and made walking very difficult. I'd pull my foot up to take a step,

but my brand-new bike shoe stayed buried. No matter how well I strapped them down, they kept getting stuck in the deep mud. I finally took off my shoes and chucked them into the jungle.

Mark had named some elements of the course with appropriately scary labels: the Trail of Fire, the Valley of Pain, and the Lost World, which was reportedly a sacred part of the jungle. According to the map, teams had the option to walk a forty-mile death march around the area, or just follow the terrain and go up and over it. Kevin and his team of race designers never imagined any team would ever really choose the up-and-over route. But we did. The jungle was so thick and so steep that we would stand on each other's shoulders to get to the next step up. Our choice put us far behind our planned schedule, but we pushed on.

Every day brought something different. We entered areas thick with bamboo and bristling vines that strangle buildings and trees and leave open wounds on everyone that gets too close to the black barbs. Machetes didn't do much to clear our paths. We managed waterfall ascents and crossed frigid rivers filled with slimy, slippery boulders.

The locals made some extra cash by offering their services to a bunch of haggard racers. We hired a strong Fijian who wanted to help us to the next checkpoint. Heading up a river, jumping and sliding from boulder to boulder, I slipped and fell on my backside. The Fijian literally picked me up with one hand and set me back upright on the boulder. The people of Fiji were not only incredibly nice, but also had amazing strength. I wasn't sitting down, so I didn't really notice anything off with my tailbone. I knew something was injured, as it was painful when I did try to sit or to sleep on my back. It was just another irritant on the list of body parts that hurt.

Fiji was just a constant test of our mental and physical wills to stay on that course. During those really difficult legs of the course, I imagined all of the things I would do to Mark if I saw him in a dark alley. Kevin and Scott were next on my imaginary list.

On the seventh day, we finally came across our gearboxes, holding food and extra clothes. We thought we'd find them every couple of days; we didn't and made do with what we had. The food was comforting and nice, but we literally had hours left before the finish line. I gobbled down some fruit-in-a-cup and dumped my tennis shoes, the ones worn on the slippery boulders, into the trash, never wanting to see them again. During a lengthy race like this your feet are a wreck, your skin is a mess, you have cuts, bruises, insect bites. No one gets out unscathed, but exhaustion and hunger are the real nemesis to a racer.

We rappelled down a steep cliff on the last day, knowing we were close to the finish line. At the bottom of the rappel, Marshall slipped on a rock but fortunately wasn't injured. Checking on Marshall, Mark Macy teased him that it would be a bummer if we had to drop out just before the finish line. Marshall composed himself and off we went. We arrived at the shoreline, grabbed the kayaks, and paddled our way to the finish.

Dianne Burnett had gotten a kayak from the hotel where the finish line was and paddled out to meet us as we approached the shore. Mark was there at the shoreline to greet us. All of the evil things I wanted to do to him during the race disappeared as I hugged him. It was great to see him, and we were all on cloud nine because we had finished the tough course Mark had created. Of the eighty-one teams that started, we were one of the twenty-three teams that completed the course, and we placed eleventh overall. The high, the elation of crossing the finish line, can't really be attached to words. It's a feeling, a state of mind like no other.

Dianne left her kayak and met us near the stage. She handed me a martini and then grabbed her son's half-eaten plate of French fries and gave that to me, as well. Those were the best fries I have ever had. After that, I went to the medical tent to have my sore, swollen feet checked. The doctor looked at me and felt a need to point out that this was not a good sport for people. Like the doctor in Borneo, he asked why I did this.

I just laughed. If I'd known the reason behind this affliction, I would have done something about it.

I had broken my tailbone during the race, lost twenty pounds, and had the greatest time of my life on an epic course with a remarkable team. I had so much admiration for my teammates. They were great teachers, and they not only had fun on the challenge, but they were also funny. Their humor, especially Mark Macy's quips and his secret granola recipe, kept us all smiling. There's little that can compare to the feeling of being part of a team that is not only capable, but also caring.

When a race is first over, I can't seem to eat enough. The feeling of being full can take days to come back. After Fiji ended, my roommate Charlie and I ordered breakfast in the room. When our teammates would show up, we'd go to another breakfast, followed by two lunches, and a large dinner. Eating and not feeling full was the oddest sensation.

People often ask me, "Where do you pee?" "What do you talk about?" "What if you're on your period?" "Are you afraid of the wildlife?"

I used to walk an extra hundred yards to pee in private. I quickly learned that that was a lot of wasted energy. I can squat behind my pack and pee without being noticed. Or I'd just step off the trail and pee. When you have to poop, you dig holes and bury it. Inhibition goes away after a race or two. At one point I had quite a heat rash, and the rubbing of my Lycra tights against my skin irritated my legs even more. I had a solution. I took my pants off. I don't wear underwear while racing, as it's one more thing to bother me, so I tied a shirt around my waist. That gave my thighs some fresh, dry air and no one knew a thing.

As far as conversation, all of my teammates have been pretty funny. I loved listening to them, except when the conversations turned technical or had anything to do with computers. I fully checked out and went back to designing houses in my head. I've made some great design decisions while hiking. Daydreaming about house designs can make eight hours go by in a flash. When I had fully designed my house, I'd then move on to composing houses for my kids. Another mind game I played was having conversations with friends. I'd take each friend one by one and tell them how great they were and why. Rarely did I tell them all of this when I returned home, as I didn't want them to think I was lame. If I needed to step up my pace, I would think of a topic that made me mad, and that actually made me walk faster. If I were climbing something really steep, I'd count steps to take my mind off the pain and exertion.

Snakes have always been my biggest fear. In Borneo, my team had a thirty-minute group hallucination that there was a python on the trail. We spent precious time wondering what we were going to do about it and throwing rocks and sticks at it. No matter what we threw at it, it never moved. A closer look revealed that it wasn't a snake at all. It was just twisted vines.

During a race in Sri Lanka, we had to be driven down part of the highway because there were too many elephants lingering near the road. The race designers were concerned that the huge creatures would charge the racers. Fear of the wildlife is just one of those things you add to the list of things not to think about. I prefer to think that the teams who went before us had scared away any threatening wildlife. With regard to the predators in the wild, ignorance can be bliss.

There are many mind games you can utilize to self-motivate, overcome hardships, fear, and pain, and still allow a dual focus on both activity and thought. The one thing you can't allow is for the mind to move from a cautious fearful thought to an overwhelming fearful thought. The cautious kind of fear can be a type of preparation, but out-and-out fear can be debilitating to any racer.

I returned home to more demands from my husband. I was handed a post-nuptial agreement that had to be signed by an attorney. I interviewed two or three attorneys, but none would allow me to sign the agreement. One lawyer flat-out asked me, "Why would you even want to be with someone who gave you such a mean document to sign?"

They, like numerous therapists we visited, told me I should leave him. When I refused to sign it, my husband said that we would be getting a divorce and that I needed to find somewhere else to live. So I did.

A few months later, in January, I packed the kids' toys and all of our clothes and left. I had run out of options; his anger toward me was never going to stop. He said I brought out the worst in him, but he could never tell me why. The mood swings and silent treatments were giving me horrible stomachaches. I just wanted out.

The kids and I moved into a house that I was determined I could remodel and sell. I knew that I could make decent money flipping houses. "Flip to climb" became my motto.

I was always amazed when someone would say something snarky about or to me, suggesting that I get a job and stop wandering all over the world. The IRS considered what I did to be a job, and the whole remodeling process seemed like work to me, even though I enjoyed it all tremendously. To me, the most important thing was that it gave me a sense of accomplishment. Buying, selling, and making something old and neglected new again gave me a high. I always feel like I'm making the house feel the way it did when it was new, and I like making a house feel happy. When I climb or hike or participate in any sport that requires hours of movement, I design houses in my head. Hours—even days—can seem to sail by in a shorter time frame, as I am completely lost in thought.

———

My first event after experiencing the freedom of making my own decisions was Race Across America (RAAM), a bike race from San Diego to the Atlantic City Boardwalk. I was on a team of two women and two men. Charlie Engle and Stefani Jackenthal were two of my three teammates, and the four of us would rotate in four-hour shifts. We wanted to race hard, yet we knew we weren't professional cyclists. Before the race even began, things got off to a rough start, with the team captain promising lots of money that never materialized. Thankfully, I managed to secure a small sponsor right before the race started to help defray costs.

Ella, who was twelve at the time, came along as a crewmember. She could talk for hours about anything and everything, so she was tasked with the job of keeping the driver of the RV awake through the night or on flat, boring places along the course. As we drove through one particularly flat, barren state she asked, "Why do we even own this state?"

I loved having her on this adventure, as she was always up for anything. The only time I wasn't happy with her was when she didn't wake me to see the Amish riding their horse-drawn buggies in the middle of the night. For me it represented a frozen space in time that was a part of not only our history, but also our present.

It was my turn to ride. We were just leaving Pie Town, New Mexico, and cars had started to back up on this two-lane highway on the outskirts of a barely populated ghost town. I'm on a bike, I thought. I'll just ride right through all the cars.

I caught up to our team motor home, which was stopped amid the line of cars and trucks. Ella and one of the crew were standing outside of it waiting for me. They waved me down. "Give me the bike," the crew person said, motioning to me.

"No, I'm on a bike, I'll just ride through the cars," I replied. I was taken aback by the silliness of the thought that I would give up my bike.

Ella sternly said, "Mom, get off the bike and come in here."

She asked me to climb on top of the bed that sits above the driver and passenger seats in the RV. She told me that a racer from Team Vail had

been hit and killed by a semi-trailer truck and that his father had witnessed
the accident.

I was shocked, saddened, sickened, horrified. The fact that my daughter was
exposed to all of this was heartbreaking to me. I was feeling for her and how
this might affect her when she went to gallows humor and stated that our
team had moved up a spot in the standings since Team Vail was out. I realized
that she didn't know how to process the rider's death. We talked a little, and I
hoped it would help her process the day's events. Instead, she asked me to stop
racing altogether. She didn't want me to race in anything in the future. It was
too much for her to see someone she'd just met die. I realized that she, for the
first time, understood the possible ramifications of adventure sports. I told
her the usual lie that this would be my last race. She was satisfied with that.

We were eventually given the go-ahead to continue the course. When I rode
past his crumpled-up bike and areas covered in white powder, my mind
couldn't comprehend why I was still on my bike. I wanted to quit. I dialed my
cell phone from my bike and Lynn answered. I told her what had happened
and how I was feeling. She told me to put my head down and just focus on
riding, to be safe, and to not quit. So, I didn't. She knew how to motivate me to
finish the race.

It was a difficult race. We biked through traffic, rainstorms, heat, and tornado
warnings, and every time I got off the bike, I'd stick a frozen water bottle down
my bike shorts because my private parts were so swollen.

We had a police escort keeping traffic behind us on the New Jersey Turnpike
as we rode four abreast to the finish line. It was an incredible experience, and
yet I felt really bad for the people caught up in traffic behind us.

We crossed the finish line six days, thirteen hours, and thirty-three minutes
after we left San Diego, winning our division and placing second overall. I
felt like I really got to see the country during RAAM, but swore I was finished
with racing and dangerous sports. It was the same hollow promise that I
asserted after every tortuous event.

———

The year before the divorce papers were filed and I moved out, my husband and I had signed up to climb Mount Elbrus, the highest peak in Europe, located in the Caucasus Range in Russia. The kids and I were living in our own house now, so making the climb separately made more sense.

One of us would be with the children while the other climbed. My soon-to-be-official ex insisted on climbing the mountain first. When he returned from Russia, he drove straight to my new house to drop off his duffle bag with the expectation that I would wash everything for him. He also left me a Nalgene bottle full of his urine that he hadn't emptied after the climb. It seemed that he failed to understand the concept of separation.

I left the next day for my turn at Mount Elbrus. As I sat at LAX waiting for my flight to board, he called. He wanted me back. I couldn't believe it.

I just wanted to climb and told him so. I had just finished my first remodel and was getting settled in with my kids in their new home and our new living situation. I had zero interest in meeting or dating anyone. I simply wanted the freedom and enjoyment of climbing Elbrus.

Then I saw him. He was standing on a train platform in Moscow. My immediate thought upon first laying eyes on Todd was, *Oh no*. I had never believed in the fairy-tale of love at first sight. That is, until it happened to me. I turned away from him to speak with someone else. I was trying to ignore him, but I knew in my soul that I was going to be with this man. I was smitten.

I got to know him as we did various training hikes. It was necessary to acclimatize to the altitude, so we made several pre-climbs to help that along.

We ascended the southern route to the western summit, the highest peak of the twin cones. The extinct volcano was covered in snow and reached an elevation of 18,510 feet. At one of the camps on the way up, we were all to practice our ice skills with our "sharps." I left the small hut we were gathered in and went to a few tents to grab people's ice axes and crampons. With a small handful of each in both hands, I began walking back to the hut. The next thing I knew, without any thought, I threw everything up in the air and dove into the snow.

Lightning struck a rock within twenty feet of me. My head had been a bit tingly while collecting the sharps and I had ignored the odd sensation, as I had no idea why that was happening. After I stood back up, my hair was a complete mess, and I had a raging headache. Training was cancelled.

A day or so later, we were on our way to the summit. There was a more technical aspect to this summit compared to Kili or Mount Whitney. Ice axes and crampons helped us traverse ice cliffs and glacial ice-covered slopes. I'll never forget carefully hiking down to an outhouse that dangled precariously over the side of a cliff. Elbrus seemed to me to be one big dirty pit. I was not awed or inspired by the beauty of this mountain.

During one training hike, Todd said I would have no problem climbing Mount Everest. That was a game-changer for me. Having the owner of one of the most successful climbing companies in the world tell you that you are capable definitely plants the seed in your head. Training for the Seven Summits wouldn't be anything more than I was already doing, and there would probably be fewer injuries. Plus, I'd get to sleep in a warm, comfortable tent and eat regularly. At the moment these climbs, although technical, sounded like a vacation compared to adventure racing. That small bit of encouragement was all I needed to add the Seven Summits to the list of sports I wanted to do.

High up on the mountain, we camped for the night near some old army barrels. My ex told me that he'd left a note hidden in one of them, told me where and said that I should retrieve it. I found it and shook my head as I read the words that told of how he'd thought the grass would be greener if he divorced me. He'd discovered it wasn't, and now he wanted me back. By the time I walked onto the summit of Mount Elbrus, I thought, *Hell no! I will never ever go back.*

Standing on the summit, I felt the remarkable realization that I was almost divorced, thrilled about that freedom, setting a trajectory for the remaining summits, and I had a new love in my life.

I had a few months to train before the Panama Rainforest Extreme, another expedition race. That would also give my children and me time to settle into a new life and lifestyle. The kids were initially upset when we told them of the separation. Ella went into, "How does this affect me and what can I get out of it?" mode. I thought that was rather healthy. Johnny was furious with his dad, wouldn't speak to him, and refused to go to his house. Olivia was still young enough to be a mommy's girl; she didn't care about the separation. She was only five, and just wanted to be with me or with her friends.

It's fascinating how you can have three children with the same parents, and yet each one can be so very different. Ella had to have a fully scheduled day when she was young, Johnny didn't like leaving the house and just wanted to play with his friends, and Olivia needed to know what the day was going to look like before we even had breakfast. They were settling into the new routines and, even though I knew it was difficult for them, I knew it would be good for them and me, too. Happy children come from happy parents.

However, I was still feeling like a failure as a wife and mother. I hadn't lived up to the antiquated social constructs that I'd made such a priority. I couldn't be the dutiful wife with no outside interests, nor could I repress the desire to race and climb. And I wasn't the Kool-Aid-commercial mom who always had a smile, neatly coifed hair, and a happy group of ideal children around the pitcher with the smile on it. The only part of the Kool-Aid commercial that resembled my reality was the house-full-of-kids part.

The kids' and my first trip without their dad was to a dude ranch in Wyoming, a few hours outside of the Grand Teton National Park, during their summer break. I wanted the kids to have as much fun as possible to make up for my perceived failures. The kids invited a couple of friends, and we flew to Salt Lake City, rented a fifteen-passenger van, and drove to Wyoming. We stayed in Jackson Hole for a few nights, where we met up with a friend and her three kids. The ten of us went river rafting and signed up with a local company to take us "climbing." The kids were able to do some basic rock climbing and rappelling, which they seemed to enjoy. They were getting the basics down, but Johnny and one of the girls wanted a bit more, so we arranged a private climb for them the following day.

No matter what I was doing, I couldn't help but look out to Grand Teton. This iconic granite peak beckoned me. I asked one of the guides if we could climb it really quickly before we all left for the dude ranch. He said that most people take two days, but he agreed that we could give it a try. I made arrangements for the children to be occupied while I made a quick summit of the stunning mountain. Johnny wanted to climb with me and, to appease him, I promised we would come back so he could climb it as well. I understood that he wanted to conquer the Grand as much as I did. But my idea was to be back that afternoon to meet up with everyone for the evening's activities. I wanted it to be a fast climb.

My guide, Forrest McCarthy, met me in the hotel lobby around midnight, and we drove to the trailhead. It was exhilarating to be helmeted up and back on an ascent. The rock is gorgeous, the views incredible, and the climb challenging. It could be a little hairy if you lost your footing or fell. That gave it just enough of an edge to make it exciting. It was all the things I loved about climbing. And I made it up and back in one day.

It was a perfect trip. The kids had a blast and tried new things, and I got to have an incredible climb. Johnny informed me that he'd been watching paragliders jump off one of the peaks. It really sparked his sense of adventure and his childhood dream of flying. I found the sport boring and couldn't fully understand what he found so fascinating about it. I guess we never truly know what our kids are thinking when they see something new or how it will affect them, but I could tell this was something Johnny wanted to experience.

The Panama Rainforest Extreme race was on my calendar for late in the year. I loved jungle racing, despite what it did to my feet, and was excited about this one. I was racing with a highly regarded US team made up of Eco-Challenge veterans: Nick Moore, Jack Dunn, and Jack's friend, Louis. Because each of us had been involved with so many races, we were favored to win this one.

The opening race briefing was the usual, nothing we hadn't heard before, except for the bit about crocodiles and caimans. The race director was adamant that no teams were to be in the river past a certain hour because of the dangerous predators. We agreed and were off to hike, bike, climb, and paddle across Panama. I remember the beauty of the raindrops on the lake as we paddled across it in a gentle rain. Back on land, the terrain made it a typical jungle race. Everything was green, muddy, and potentially dangerous, so we decided to move to the river, because it's easier to maneuver through water than through the tangled maze that covered the hillsides.

We continued downstream as the sun began to set, casting eerie shadows throughout the primeval forest. We didn't want to admit we were lost and wandering around the jungle in the river. The later it got, the more I recalled the warnings to be safely out of the water. The later it got, the more the race director's words screamed in my head. We were doing exactly what he had said not to do. I was wet, cold, angry, and scared, and again vowed to myself that this would be my last race. I actually meant it this time.

We finally got out of the river and tried to negotiate the harsh landscape, which rose from and fell away into deep canyons. Nick, our team captain and navigator, declared us lost by eleven p.m., which was the time when we should have been crossing the finish line. Instead, we had been hopelessly wandering around in the jungle for hours. Everything was slick and overgrown to the point that it was difficult to make out what was around you.

Reluctantly, we pulled out the emergency phone and GPS that had been provided by the race organizers and turned them on. The phone had one bar of battery strength left and the GPS couldn't give us our coordinates, as the steep jungle walls blocked its receiver. We were able to get through to the organizers but were nervous because we didn't know how long the battery would last. They were adamant that we stay where we were and said they would find us. To help identify our location, they asked us to send up one of our emergency flares. We sent up two. They couldn't see them.

At one point, Nick fell off a cliff, only to be saved from serious injury by a sturdy tree branch. After he crawled back up from his fall, we decided to sleep until daylight and proceed from there. We spooned to stay warm—I called the middle to have more warmth between two teammates. Neither of them was producing any body heat. We were out of food and water. We were sopping wet from the rain and shivering violently. This was the first time, in all of the extreme events I'd participated in, that I had the thought that I might never see my children again.

Morning finally broke over the hills, and we turned the emergency phone on to call in. They again told us to stay put, that they would find us. Jack vetoed the idea and said, "Bullshit. They will never find us. We have to get ourselves out of here."

As a young child, I saw a movie in which a teenage girl was the sole survivor of a plane crash in a jungle. She had remembered someone telling her that if she was ever lost, to follow water, even a trickle, as it would lead to bigger water, and eventually to people. That's exactly what we did. We followed a very small creek that got bigger and bigger. By that afternoon, we hit pavement. I literally got down on my hands and knees and kissed it. Within minutes, the police and an ambulance were there for us.

The military had been out all night searching for the four Americans lost in the Panamanian jungle. We were all fine and were transported by ambulance straight to our hotel. One of the military guys had asked us, "Who was breaking branches as you walked?"

I responded, "I was. I do that when I walk sometimes, not thinking."
He then asked, "Why did you stop?"
I said, "Because my hands were getting so torn up. I just stopped doing it."

He said that his team had been following those branches hoping to find us, and then they just stopped. We thanked them over and over for coming to our rescue and headed to our rooms. Jack and I shared a room, showered, jumped into our beds, and ordered cheeseburgers. It was not lost on me that within a twenty-four-hour period, I had gone from thinking I was going to die to eating a cheeseburger while propped up on fluffy pillows. There's an amalgamation of emotional peaks and valleys that propel you forward when you survive something. It's a combination of elation that you're alive, relief that the ordeal is over, the letdown from the adrenaline rush, and the comforting knowledge that you will be seeing your family in a couple of days that gets you through a harrowing, less-than-satisfactory experience.

———

I had barely gotten home, and we were off again. It was the holiday season and, even though my ex and I were living in separate homes, we took the kids to Cabo San Lucas with a group of friends. It was a relaxing trip that focused on the kids having a great time during their first Christmas with divorced parents.

We were all playing on the beach when I sat down on my friend's beach blanket to watch her and her son play Uno. All of a sudden, the blanket seemed to swirl, and I fainted. I lay on the blanket burning up with a fever, feeling awful. I guess people thought I was drunk or hung over even though, with three kids, I didn't drink much and hadn't had a hangover since college. One hotel guest referred to me as the "drunk blond on the beach." Some friends helped me move closer to the water to cool off. Then they moved me again into the shade of a wall.

My fever was high and I could barely walk. I was so achy I thought I had a bad flu virus. I could feel every cell of my body, and it felt like ice picks stabbing me all over. It was pain like I have never felt. My eyeballs felt like they were on fire.

Ella wanted to go horseback riding and was angry that I wanted to go to my room first. Fortunately, my ex said he would take the kids riding so I could sleep, but Johnny refused to leave me. Johnny helped me into a cold bath to try to get my temperature down and helped me out of the tub and into bed. I was embarrassed that my young son saw me naked and practically immobile but was grateful he hadn't left me.

We were scheduled to fly home the next day, Christmas Day. During the night my fever finally broke, which left the bed sopping wet and me exhausted. The plane was thankfully half-empty, allowing me to put the armrests up and sleep across three seats during the flight. When we landed, I turned on my cell phone and discovered numerous missed calls from my Panama teammates. They all either were in the hospital or had just been released. They had leptospirosis and were wondering if I had it, too.

I probably should have been in a hospital, because leptospirosis is a serious bacterial infection that is usually caused by contaminated water getting in your eyes, nose, mouth, or broken skin. It can cause a wide range of symptoms, and everyone on my team was suffering to some degree. I was mentally done with racing. Between the alligators, race directors who couldn't find us even when we shot off flares, and the overall trauma imposed on my body and mind, I was done with adventure racing.

Climbing the Seven Summits seemed like a much safer situation.

Chapter 5

Mt. Vinson, Antarctica

I had less than two weeks to recover from the debacle of leptospirosis before I had to be on a plane to Ushuaia, Argentina, to meet my fellow Vinson climbers. This would be the third climb with Alpine Ascents and my third of the Seven Summits. I still felt weak and shaky but was improving a bit every day. I wasn't sure how the climb would go in my depleted state, but I was determined to meet the challenge.

Before any of us could fly down to the ice, we had a lengthy meeting with the flight company that oversaw all of the logistics for the plane and the camp where we would be staying. When it was time for questions, one of our team asked in dead seriousness if there would be an outlet for his blow dryer. I couldn't believe it. I have climbed with some divas, but this took the cake. People turned around in their chairs to gawk at him; his expressionless face didn't give away the fact that this was the start of his nonstop humor.

We were told that the flight to the ice is dependent on many things. The weather played the biggest part in determining when we could leave. The pilots had to know that the weather would still be clear four hours after our departure from Argentina when we landed in Antarctica. If we had to turn around for any reason, the company would lose a tremendous amount of money. It was best for them to be certain we faced no obstacles during the flight.

After the presentation, several of us stayed behind to talk. There were rumors that the plane, a Russian-built Ilyushin, was stolen. I had no idea if that was true, but a picture of Muammar Gaddafi hung proudly on the wall just outside of the cockpit door. That was a little scary. The pilots also had to be sober before the flight, and that was something that couldn't be guaranteed.

After a couple of days of delay, we finally boarded the behemoth of a plane and settled in jump seats facing each other. Our gear and other supplies were stacked down the middle of the plane, front to back and in the cargo area at the rear of the plane.

Curious, I lifted one of the blankets covering all of that gear and saw fuel barrels. Holy hell, I thought, envisioning the explosion that would occur if we crashed. Some mattresses were thrown on top of the gear and barrels and, as soon as we took off, some of the passengers climbed on top to get a little sleep. I chatted with some of my climbing mates and thought about our upcoming landing on ice in a plane full of fuel. At some point, someone started to explain how the airplane doesn't use brakes when it lands. They compared it to driving on snow and ice. If you apply the brakes, you might skid or even flip the vehicle. A normal flight that doesn't land on a blue-ice runway can use both the brakes and the reverse thrust of the engines. But on blue ice, the pilots only use reverse thrust to come to a stop. It suddenly dawned on me that just getting there was probably more dangerous than the climb. I reminded myself that, unless the pilots were suicidal, we'd be fine. Then I thought about all of the fuel barrels lined up, covered with blankets and mattresses. We were going to land a big plane full of flammable liquid, on a blue-ice runway, without using brakes. I reminded myself to breathe.

We bounced a little when we first touched the ice. The plane felt like it might spin, but it stayed steady. It did seem to take forever to come to a halt, at which point I exhaled. We sat for a minute, then suddenly the back end of the plane opened and began to lower. It was like being in a sci-fi movie. The whiteness of the landscape was blinding as we slowly walked down the ramp onto the ice. This was January, and sunlight reflected on the glaringly white wilderness twenty-four hours a day. I loved it. I function on daylight, not so much the dark.

As we moved across the glaze of white, the ice sounded like china plates breaking with every step. It was an oddly beautiful sound that, to me, seemed elegant and dainty. There was a soft crackling with every step, a sound that didn't match the harsh environment that I was viewing. I looked down and could see the ice crack under my feet. I'd never heard that sound on any other ice. I smiled and thought that maybe the satisfaction I felt from the sound was like smashing plates without actually smashing plates.

We dropped our gear in our tents before meeting in the dining hall to go over the plan for the mountain. We were told we'd be taking a small plane to the base camp of Vinson. The camp we were in now catered to everyone who was down on the ice for any reason. There were people going to the South Pole, explorers, scientists, and people who didn't share their reasons for visiting this frozen wasteland. The camp at the base of the mountain was primarily for climbers.

Words cannot express how cold it was. Thankfully, unlike the jungles I had raced in, I had the warmest clothing to protect me from the harsh elements. At one point, Zeddy Al Refai, the comedian who wanted to know if there was a place to plug in his hair dryer, shrieked in horror when he went to pee. At the top of his lungs, he informed the continent that his member had disappeared. We all laughed, but he was right. It was bitterly frigid. Even though we had the warmest gear imaginable, frostbite happened fast and affected any skin exposed to the elements.

Antarctica is not just notoriously cold, it's also dry. Even the snow is dry, and because of that it has a very high "albedo" or reflectance of light. Everything has the appearance of the brightest white imaginable.

Several in the group were climbing Vinson to prepare for the cold, harsh conditions of Mount Everest. At least five planned to be there that spring. I was a bit jealous that they were planning Everest, but I knew it wasn't my time yet. I needed a lot more experience. The training that Vinson provided was good. It gave me a greater knowledge of steep technical ice travel, but I needed more. Climbing this and then Denali would give me more of the skills and experience Everest would require.

We boarded the ski plane, and before long we were bound for the landing strip near the base camp. I looked out over the ice shelf as the Vinson Massif rose in the distance. Compared to some of the Seven Summits, Vinson was short, at just over sixteen thousand feet. It reminded me of my first climb on Mount Whitney. But there were differences, too. Vinson required ice axes, crampons, and tolerance for a frozen, dry desert. I could feel the anticipation of the climb build within me.

After another successful ice landing, we headed off to make camp. Out came the shovels and handsaws to construct ice walls to protect the tents from the wind and to dig out an area for the dining tent. The large hole we dug was big enough for the entire team to sit in for meals and for the guides to be able to cook. It looked like the pointy top part of a circus tent sitting on the ice with four to five feet of a sitting area below it. We brought in our sleeping pads to sit on. They prevented our bodies from directly touching the ice bench where we sat. Even with the pad and all our warm clothing, it was still bitterly cold on the bum.

The plan was to acclimatize for a couple of days, pack our things into our humongous packs, and move on to the next camp. This mountain wasn't as compelling as some. It was more the vastness of the continent and the reality of how far we were from civilization. The remoteness of the location never strayed far from my mind. I wasn't yet worried about the getting-home part; I was fully focused on the climb and pleased that we were headed up the Branscomb glacier.

When you climb, you can carry heavy packs, pull sleds, or do whatever is needed so you have the proper gear. The movement helps keep your body warm even in the chilling cold. Weight is always a consideration, but nothing like the weight issues in adventure racing. On a mountain, I've never cut the handle off my toothbrush or avoided packing an extra layer because it added ten ounces. I have never brought a camera onto a racecourse. No luxuries when racing. Weight slows you down and impedes speed and mobility. By contrast, mountaineering is a slow plod. You can afford yourself some luxuries like a camera or a toothbrush handle.

A couple of days later, we moved our camp higher up the mountain. This would be our final camp before our summit attempt. Again, it was bitterly cold, and after pulling sleds and carrying a really heavy pack, we had to, once again, build snow walls and saw a large hole in the ice for our dining tent. It was exhausting but necessary work. After a night or two at this camp, we left for the top. The ascent was thankfully uneventful, except for watching for crevasses and dealing with the cold.

We reached the summit, and I made a mental note checking off the third of the seven. I had scored another personal achievement, and it felt good. I looked out across the expanse of white. I hadn't realized how beautifully colorful the world naturally is until the only thing I could see was white sprinkled with a little brown and gray from protruding rocks. This was a unique climb because of the lack of color. The vast emptiness can leave one feeling threatened and isolated, even when surrounded by fellow climbers.

At one point on the descent, I really had to poop. Usually, I am constipated on these trips, but someone had shared some salmon jerky with me. It didn't sit well, and I had to go and go now. Because of the crevasses, we were wearing harnesses and roped together. I fought it as long as I could, but finally gave in and announced that I really had to poop. People were gracious and looked away as I pulled out a large ziplock and took the smelliest dump of my life. I looked down and saw a thin crack in the ice that was very close to my feet. I was suddenly struck by the frightening thought that a crevasse might open up and swallow me in mid-poop! I quickly finished, moved away from the crack in the ice, and stuck the ziplock into another small opaque bag that I hung on the outside of my pack. I vowed never to eat salmon jerky again.

Getting onto the ice from Ushuaia, Argentina, was easy, compared to getting a return flight back to the South American city. We were safely at the main base camp, but the weather was not cooperating for the plane to fly in and get us. Looking back, I am sure the plane was only delayed by three to five days. While there, every day felt like a week. Complete lack of control of one's travel really gets to most people. I had planned the trip so that I could be back for the party I was throwing for Olivia's seventh birthday. It would be her first birthday in our new house, and I wanted it to be a happy, memorable day. Time was getting tight. I used my satellite phone to call some of the party people to confirm everything. The jump house was scheduled, the cake ordered, and all the accoutrements needed for a kid's birthday were in place. Everything was ready—except Mom. I kept praying to be there on time.

Most of us were going stir-crazy wondering when we would get off the ice. I looked around at all of the type A personalities who are normally in charge of everything. Here, their titles, salaries, and positions meant nothing. They were just bodies on the ice waiting to go home. I overheard one frustrated man say he had friends in the military and he was going to call them to come get him. Others wanted to see if they could fly to the coast and take a boat home. It was all wishful thinking; the only thing we could truly do was exercise patience and, of course, try to have a little fun while we waited.

Forrest, my guide up the Teton, was one of the guides for this climb. We decided to go exploring and wound up at a mostly buried and deserted military base. We saw the tip of the roof of one of the pods peeking out from beneath the snow and ice. Forrest pulled out his Leatherman and unscrewed the vent. Once it was open we climbed down into the pod. What a surreal sight, just like everything else in Antarctica. It looked as though the people would return any moment to take up their daily activities. It seemed like they had had two seconds to stop whatever they were doing and leave. Everything was still in place. Cereal boxes sat opened on the table with the grains in the bowls, waiting to be eaten. It was like stepping back in time, into a frozen snapshot of life under the ice. It was eerily bizarre. I wondered why they had all left. We climbed back out of the vent hole, sealed it up, and didn't tell anyone what we had done.

Living in constant sunlight messes with your body clock. It was impossible to tell if it was day or night. One day our guides had gone to a party of some sort and left our group to our own devices. Some of us decided to venture into the underground storage area that was off-limits. We wanted to have a look and were surprised at what we found. Food! An airplane! So much was hidden under the ice.

I felt oddly relieved when I saw the plane. I added it into my escape-from-Antarctica plans. Each day that we couldn't fly took my mind to a darker place. Missing my daughter's birthday would have devastated me, so I envisioned stealing the plane and flying myself to the water to catch a boat. It was completely unrealistic, but you start to lose your mind when you feel like you're a prisoner with no escape.

After about a week of feeling stranded, we were given the news that the plane was on its way. We packed our things and made it down to the runway. As we stood there watching our precious flight home approach, we snapped final pictures and were grateful to finally be getting out of the white wasteland. Thankfully, I made it home in time for Olivia's party, which was my top priority.

———————

The next mountain I targeted was Denali. At 20,310 feet, it is the highest peak in North America. Vinson taught me that I could handle the cold and some technical climbing, such as the use of crampons, ropes, and ice axes. I needed to know if I could handle a higher elevation. Called "the Great One," this imposing mountain dominates the scenery as it rises over eighteen thousand feet from the base camp to the peak.

Alpine Ascents had planned a twenty-one-day trip that leaves from base camp, travels over the Kahiltna Glacier, and then begins the ascent of the West Buttress. The climb requires intermediate mountaineering skills, but the weather can be inclement and the winds powerful. Acclimatization is an absolute necessity, as it is a steep, formidable ascent. Once again, Forrest was the main guide, and he'd brought his then girlfriend, now wife, Amy, along as a co-guide. It was good to be with someone I knew and trusted.

The plane ride from Talkeetna was uneventful. It meant another ice landing, but I was getting accustomed to those. We had six climbers and three guides. At the lower camps, I shared a tent with one person. On the last camp before the summit, I shared a tent with two people. The winds on Denali were relentless. Securing our tent to the ice was of the utmost importance, and I looked at my tent mate, grateful for his weight, which I hoped would keep our tent on the mountain during the nightly winds.

I looked around at my gear. I had the required clothing, gloves, and hats—none of which were cotton, as that material takes too long to dry and will help you freeze to death if it gets wet—glacier glasses and ski goggles, and high-altitude boots. There was an ice axe and a waist leash that kept my ice axe attached to me, twelve-point mountaineering crampons, carabiners of all kinds, an alpine climbing harness that fit over my clothes and parka, and an ascender. I had a sled, sleeping pad and bag, knife, water bottles, pee bottle, and personal items, including books to occupy any downtime. I read seven novels on that climb. The last book I read, *The Trinity*, went unfinished before we flew back. It was an interesting dichotomy because, though you were with a group, you were on your own. There were no Sherpa to help carry the loads. I had to haul all of this with me.

Our small team meshed well, except for one individual. There's always one. While people were asleep in their tents, he would walk around outside, fully kitted up as if he were going to the summit that very minute. In the dining tent, another huge hole we dug into the ice complete with ice benches, he would wear his sunglasses. It was unnerving, as you never knew where he was actually looking. He was just one of those people you instinctively shy away from.

Denali was a beast. I had always imagined Everest would be the hardest mountain I would climb. Denali changed my mind on that. I hauled heavy loads on my back and pulled even heavier loads in a sled. The harness cut into my waist as I pulled the cumbersome sled. Trying to breathe slowly and calmly while climbing steep slopes was nearly impossible. At one point I prayed for a heart attack to get me off the mountain. My physical exertion was at its maximum. I had nothing left to give. The endless wind and storms that made us tent-bound for days played with my mental state, as we still hadn't had an opportunity to go to the summit. We were running out of time and weather windows.

Our team was hit with storm after storm, and it was beginning to look like we needed every one of those twenty-one days. I'd read ten pages of a book, rip them out and give them to the next person. We all needed something to occupy the downtime. We looked forward to the days when the weather permitted us to get back to the climb.

There's a section on the mountain that's appropriately called Windy Corner. The individual that most of us were trying to avoid slipped and didn't yell anything out. Climbing etiquette mandates that you yell, "Falling!" That way your rope-mates can self-arrest and hold you and them in place. Otherwise, you're all sliding down the mountain toward a huge cliff and certain death. I happened to look up as he was in mid-slide. I could feel the muscles in my body tense as I swung my axe. We were on solid blue ice, and maybe an eighth of an inch of my axe penetrated the ice. I prayed while intensely focused on those miniature teeth that gripped the frozen glaze.

"Please hold, please hold," I begged. Amy, who was behind me, saw him falling and yelled. Fortunately, the rope team arrested his fall before he dragged us all down the mountain.

Then I saw the unthinkable—he started to slide out of his harness. *He's going to drop*, I thought. Miraculously, his harness caught him at his knees. Some climbers ahead of us had witnessed the whole debacle and came down to help secure us and to get him back into his harness. All of the team was shaken by his amateur actions. He was putting all our lives in danger and, worse yet, didn't seem to care.

This was insanity. I understand the risks of climbing, and I do everything I can to keep my teammates and myself safe. I don't take unnecessary risks and I don't go past my limits. Someone else was risking my life, and I was not down for it.

After we dropped our cache of food and supplies at the upper camp and were safely back down to our lower camp, I approached one of the guides and told him, "I have three kids I need to go back home alive to. I am totally okay with quitting and going home and trying this climb at a later date because I don't trust being tied to someone who can't even put his own harness on correctly. Can I please be on another rope team?"

The guide told me that every single person had already asked the same thing, but someone had to be tied to this guy.

I couldn't understand how someone could be allowed to climb the imposing Denali with so little experience. He clearly lacked the basic skills. The director of climbing said people lied on their resumes all the time. There was nothing they could do to prevent them from climbing. I understood that, when you do anything like this, you are risking your own well-being, but to put others in harm's way was unthinkable to me. If I wasn't physically and mentally prepared for the challenge or if I didn't have the skills to accomplish the goal, I wouldn't do it.

It's really important to get along with everyone on a team. You may not like everyone, and that's all right, but you have to make an effort. For a short time, you are a tight-knit community, and you have to be able to rely on each other. Most are really great and fun and funny. Yet, there always seems to be an odd man out. The sad fact is that also can be a factor that helps a team meld together, gelling over their mutual dislike of someone. I have seen this type of group dynamic over and over. In most cases you can find one thing to bond over or agree on, and if not, as grown-ups, we just kept our mouths shut and were polite to the person. Not with this guy. While no one ever called him out, I don't think he truly bonded with anyone on this climb.

During some downtime, I made my daily call to the kids. I was missing them so much and needed to hear their voices. Johnny answered. The girls were spending the night at friends' houses and Johnny was home alone late at night. He didn't know where his dad was. I felt sad and wanted to go home to him that minute. The guilt of being away from my kids was brutal. Every phone call home delivered a gut punch. Olivia begged me to come home each time I spoke with her. I felt so torn apart by the guilt of being a nonconformist mom and an insatiable need to climb. I wondered when—if—this agony in my soul would end. The dichotomy of having two loves was tortuous. Why on Earth couldn't I be a normal mom who just wanted to stay home and bake cookies? I hated myself at times, and yet, I couldn't stop climbing.

As much as my kids complained and told me how awful I was for climbing, I had heard from other moms that they bragged to their friends about my climbs. The first time I heard that they were proud of what I did, I wanted to cry with relief. Even though my absence was difficult for them, I felt that maybe this impacted them in a good way, too. After all, I was an anorexic housewife, wannabe arm candy, who, despite numerous fears, got her act together and pursued her big, crazy dreams. I hoped they could realize their own unlimited boundaries and dreams and pursue them as I had.

The following week, most of our team reached the summit. Only one didn't make it to the top of Denali. I was roped with my tent mate, a former military man, and our guide, Trevor. Again, that sensation of accomplishment pulsed through me. And again I thought of my next climb: Everest.

On the way down from the summit, my tent mate collapsed. Because of that, the guide short-roped him from behind. Short-roping is pulling the rope and climber in, so that instead of being ten to twenty feet apart, they were right behind each other. Doing this allows the guide to keep you from falling because they can quickly grab you and break the fall.

The ascent is often viewed as the most dangerous part of a climb, but getting off a mountain can be just as treacherous. I had climbed and worked with a beautiful guide named Suzanne who died on Denali because one man tripped on the way down and pulled the entire rope team off the mountain with him.

With my tent mate short-roped in, I took the lead going down. It took an additional three to four hours to get back to camp. At one point I went slightly off-trail and found myself in thigh deep snow. I was exhausted, and to make matters worse, I was only about fifty feet from my tent when I caught my crampon on my down pants. Feathers flew everywhere. The descent was anything but smooth, and I was thankful we arrived safely back at camp.

On another leg of the descent, I ended up tied to the person who shouldn't have ever been on Denali. I was overly cautious, as I didn't want to end this successful venture with an unnecessary accident. We swapped him between teams so no one had to deal with him all the time. In one of the final stretches down the mountain, Forrest ended up tied in front of him. Our heavy sleds were sliding down the mountain in front of us, and this guy either couldn't or wouldn't control his sled.

You have to be focused on keeping the rope from your waist/harness taut in front of you so as not to let the sled ram into the ankles of the person in front of you. It happens once to almost everyone, and then they don't ever let it happen again. When you're hit by a sled, it feels like a full shopping cart smashing into your lower leg and ankles. The pain can be so severe it drops you to the ground. This person who didn't seem to care about anyone else ran his sled into the normally calm Forrest one too many times.

I'd never seen Forrest angry. He was one of the most tranquil individuals I knew, but he lost it. Forrest untied his rope, turned to the man, and said he couldn't take it anymore. Forrest switched ropes with me and tied back in. I think Forrest knew I'd had it with this guy's antics and would have done more than just untie myself from his rope if he let his sled ram into me. I was not as cool and collected as Forrest.

Denali was the hardest mountain I'd ever climbed. The weather, the guy on the team who shouldn't have been there, and the weight we had to carry and pull by sled all contributed to the difficulty. Our packs were so heavy that at one point—just as in the movie *Wild*—I put my pack on and promptly fell over backward because of the weight! None of that mattered now. My mind was already moving forward to my next climb—Everest.

———

I saw Todd briefly when we landed in Talkeetna. I missed him terribly when I was in California or on a climb. It seemed I was always torn between people and sports. In our short time together, I told him I was ready for Everest. He agreed.

Back in California, I'd drop the kids off at school and then train, Monday through Friday. Every day was different and always fun because my goal was to summit Everest. I hiked with a heavy pack up and down the Zuma View trail in Malibu all the way to Buzzards Roost, each time trying to beat my last time by at least a minute. I also rode my mountain bike up and down this trail with the same goal of being one minute faster than the last time. The children were not pleased that I was planning to climb Everest. They were never happy when I left to participate in a sport, yet they never complained if their dad went on a climb and was gone for weeks at a time. I promised I'd be home by June 1. That seemed to comfort them.

I was feeling stronger than ever physically. I was also very much in love with Todd, and any excuse to be with him was a good one. What could be better than to be together on Everest? I knew we'd have at least two weeks to share, as he would walk me to base camp, stay a night or two, and then return to Alaska. He had already climbed the mountain the Tibetans call *Chomolungma* nine times. He wasn't interested in a tenth trip up.

Being cold was my nemesis, and I didn't want anything like my experience in Panama to happen again. I knew how debilitating the cold was for me. I had an eight-thousand-meter suit custom-made with extra fill so I wouldn't be cold. My team had five women on it and numerous men. One of the women had recently been married and her husband accompanied her to base camp. I thought that was romantic. Being with Todd was wonderful. We spent ten days walking into base camp to acclimatize and cuddled under big down sleeping bags at night. I was in heaven.

We settled into our little area of base camp, and for the next six weeks, half of my focus was centered on climbing Everest. The other half was all about Todd. We had daily training jaunts up and down the mountain, walks around base camp, ladder technique training, and practice on ladders set up in base camp. We participated in a puja ceremony where we blessed our ice axes and crampons and asked for safety on the mountain. We were well on our way to our summit attempt.

I got really nauseous for a few days in base camp, as something was going around. I felt lethargic; all I wanted to do was be with Todd. Mentally, it wasn't my time to be on that mountain, but I didn't recognize it at that time. I had never been in love like this. Todd didn't judge me on my sports. He didn't judge me on anything. He was supportive of most everything, although he often commented about the lunacy of adventure racing. He couldn't understand racing and thought it was ridiculous that anyone would do that to themselves. At this point, I was done with racing and focused almost exclusively on climbing. I knew that unless you'd experienced adventure racing, you couldn't explain it. We continued to soak up the sublime ambience of the mountain, hike, and talk. It was beyond wonderful to have that time with Todd.

After being in base camp for four weeks, we were finally ready to go to Camp Three for the first time. We would spend one night there before returning to Camp One. At this point my mindset was still in race mode—I had to get somewhere fast and hopefully first. It was an instinctive feeling of wanting to pass anyone I saw in front of me. That is an adventure racer's attitude: see them, reel them in, and pass them. There couldn't be a worse mindset while climbing. Going up the Lhotse Face without oxygen, I pushed myself to pass whoever was on the rope in front of me. What I should have done was keep my head down, take my time, focus on slow, steady, and calm breathing, and most importantly, ignore anyone in front of me.

Before I knew it, I was lying down on my face, wanting to take a five-minute nap. I was struggling to breathe. At one point I looked up at the sky and saw so many trees that I was convinced I was in Central Park. I told myself my kids would be fine without me—they had their dad. *They'll be okay*, I kept telling myself. I wasn't aware of what was real and what wasn't.

Tony, one of my climbing mates, kicked me with his crampons on. The sharp jolt against my body refocused my thoughts. He told me to get up and keep going. He reminded me that I had done much harder things than walking up this sheet of ice.

I snapped out of my Central Park daydream and, with Tony's help, I made it to C3. I was still struggling to breathe and was given oxygen as soon as I got into a tent. I didn't like the mask that covered my face. Even though it was providing lifesaving oxygen, I felt like I was suffocating. I started clawing at the side of the tent, similarly to the way a drowning person grabs onto the person trying to save them.

After about fifteen minutes, I was able to calm my breathing down and function without the oxygen. My brain began to clear, and I could process rational thoughts again. This was a huge lesson for me. On the next time up the mountain, I would pull my baseball cap down low on my forehead and focus on nothing but my feet, my ascender on the rope, and my breath. I would not look at anyone in front of me. I would take it slow and steady. Climbing Everest isn't a race. No one wins for being on the summit or into camp first. I felt like the majestic mountain had taught me a valuable lesson and gave it a lot of thought as we headed back down her icy slopes.

The newlywed on our team had decided to start hooking up with another one of our climbers. I was frustrated with them. It created an awkward base camp experience. For some reason people think that you can't hear them if they are in a tent when, in reality, everyone can hear everything. This cohabitation unsettled the Sherpa, as this is a huge no-no on this mountain. It's considered disrespectful of the mountain and she showed her anger over it with numerous storms and avalanches. This was more than a superstition. It was a way of life. It was an innate understanding and appreciation of the power of the mountain, whom you show respect to by never sleeping with your feet pointed toward her. On our summit attempt we had to turn around at Camp Two because severe storms were predicted. The mountain was not happy.

A few climbers dropped out, and I had a choice to make. I could stay and hope for another summit attempt, or I could go home and stick to the promise I had made to my kids before I left. The weather was getting warmer, and the possibility of ice screws coming loose was a serious consideration. Ice screws anchor the ropes, and therefore the climbers, to the mountain. Other weather-related factors were in play, too. Snowstorms, whiteouts, and avalanches made summer climbs dangerous. No one had ever summited that late, and yet they were still willing to sit and wait for clear weather.

My friend Lynn Jacob had hiked to base camp to help me celebrate the summit. Instead, she arrived to find me contemplating my choices. There was really no choice. I had to keep my word to my kids. They needed to know that if I said something, I meant it. I needed my kids to trust me when I made a promise about things such as return times. I called Todd on my satellite phone and told him I would be leaving. He begged me to reconsider and told me it would haunt me the rest of my life if I left.

A day or two after I got home, I heard that the team had indeed summited. Todd was right. It did haunt me. To make matters worse, I went to a fundraiser shortly upon my return as a guest of a close friend. To my left were a supermodel and her tequila maker husband. My friend told them that I had just returned from attempting Mount Everest. She asked what kind of mother leaves her kids for two months to climb. I felt another blow of defeat. Then I remembered seeing her in some magazine on some yacht. Her children were probably home with a nanny while she partied. I realized it was all about perspectives and priorities. Snide comments from people always left me shaking my head. When I was home, I was fully home. I rarely went out with friends at night and considered the time from school pick-up until the next morning at school drop-off to be sacred kid time. Years ago, another mom told me that she ran all of her errands while the kids were in school and when they weren't in school, all her time was devoted to her kids. I tried to emulate that as much as possible. I realized these people don't climb, so they don't get the passion involved with it. That was their problem of perspective, not mine. I wasn't living my life for random people's approval. The only opinions that mattered to me were my children's.

The good side of coming home early was that I could spend more time with the kids. Johnny had wanted to climb Kili and he'd already conquered Mount Vinson, one of the Seven Summits, with his dad. He begged to go, and I always knew that someday I would take my kids. Johnny wanted to go before the girls, as he now had the Seven Summits on the brain. The girls were occupied with friends and summer camps, so I agreed to climb Kilimanjaro with Johnny.

There was a cute teenage girl on the climb with us. It was nice for Johnny to have someone close to his age to hang out with. During the day, Johnny walked mostly with the porters and not the rest of us. They taught him to play hacky-sack and spent hours in conversation with him as he adored them, and toward the end of the trip one of them said to him, "Don't become like the rest of the white men." Johnny promised that he wouldn't. I had watched men on my various climbs and assumed the porters were telling Johnny to stay caring and happy. Johnny lived up to his word. His heart remained open to everyone. He knew no strangers.

The kid was so strong that one of the women on the trip asked him to carry a full Nalgene to the top for her so she'd have extra water. He agreed to help her out. At Stella Point, Johnny wasn't feeling 100 percent. I told him to drink her water. He had carried it; he could drink it. I thought that was only fair. He took a few sips of the water with electrolytes and refused any more.

I didn't take Johnny on safari after the climb because I knew he would be bouncing off the walls if he had to sit all day. We flew in, we climbed, and we flew home. We were door-to-door in nine days. I was so proud of him.

The climbs in those early teenage years set him up for bigger climbs as he got older. They kept him busy and gave him the perfect excuse to not do drugs. When his friends were getting high, he would politely decline. "I have a climb coming up and I can't mess up my lungs." A parent, whose house the kids were all getting high at, told me that everyone was high but Johnny.

I took Johnny back to Jackson to climb the Grand as I had promised the year before. It was sketchy enough to excite him, and it was also fun. The ropes, helmets, harnesses, gave him a chance to become more comfortable with the paraphernalia. I knew Johnny would have a great time whether we summited or not.

Forrest McCarthy was once again the guide. He was a good friend by now, but he wasn't sure about someone as young as Johnny doing the climb in a day. As a favor to me, he was willing to give it a go. Forrest was surprised when we succeeded in the quick turnaround. Johnny did a great job, even though he suffered a little altitude sickness—a headache—on the saddle coming down. It was a good reminder to him that his mother was strong and fit and not ready to be passed up by her young son. Not just yet anyway.

Chapter 6

Yak Trek in Alaska, the Grand Teton

Johnny decided that he wanted to climb the Seven Summits. In 2004, his dad was planning to climb Mount Vinson and offered to take our twelve-year-old son along. He wasn't even out of middle school, but I had seen him climb and knew he would be capable of climbing Vinson. It would be different for him, much colder than the Teton and a more technical climb. I agreed that he could go.

On the way up, one of his guides, Vern Tejas, told him stories about paragliding from the summit. Johnny had been enthralled with paragliding from the time he was nine and had convinced a babysitter to let him fly tandem with a pilot. There is no age requirement for tandem glides, and to solo requires maturity rather than a specific number of years you've spent on the planet.

With dreams of gliding off the mountain, Johnny and his dad reached the summit days after his thirteenth birthday. He was the youngest person to ever do so and set a world record that can never be broken because the minimum legal age to climb Vinson was later raised to sixteen. He had conquered two of the Seven Summits—Kilimanjaro and Vinson—by the time he was thirteen.

I was involved in a custody battle with my ex that was taking all my energy. At the advice of my attorney, I stopped participating in climbing and racing events and set my focus on being a traditional, stay-at-home mom.

"Good mothers don't leave their children to climb mountains and race," I was told. It made no difference that my ex was doing the same climbs and races. The attorneys felt the courts would view my settled-down lifestyle more favorably than that of a mountain-climbing, racing athlete who split her time between adventuring and being a mom. The double standard for women and moms was alive and well. There was never any doubt in my mind that I could do both. I did a few small things, but nothing that would interfere with the perception they wanted before the court.

While I was concerned with custody issues, court dates, and how I presented myself, Johnny got a paraglider and began taking lessons in Malibu. He had a wonderful instructor, but the one good spot they could land on was on a beach parallel to the Pacific Coast Highway. The lifeguards discouraged him from landing on the beach by telling him it was too dangerous, that he could injure someone on the beach, and that he was startling drivers on the highway. Eventually they told him that they'd have him arrested if he did it again.

He and his instructor moved their operation to continue the lessons, but Johnny crashed into some trees on a hillside. He wasn't severely injured, but it was enough for him to decide that paragliding could wait until he was eighteen. In the meantime, he wanted to climb the remaining five of the Seven Summits and climb to raise awareness of two causes dear to his heart: genocide and Parkinson's disease.

I missed climbing. It was a huge part of my life. While on a trek in the wilderness of Alaska, I was introduced to a friend of Todd's who knew about my legal/custody issues. He also knew that I had stopped climbing based on my attorney's suggestion to be a more respectable mom. With a deep southern drawl, he said, "Your ex-husband is going to harass you whether you do or whether you don't, so you might as well do, and have yourself a good time."

And with those sage words, I decided to climb Carstensz Pyramid in West Papua. The 16,023-foot peak requires basic rock-climbing skills and knowledge of rappelling and jumaring, which is a technique used to ascend ropes. It's a moderately difficult climb of the highest mountain in the region of Oceania.

There are two Seven Summits lists. One includes the West Papua mountain that includes Carstensz Pyramid, and one includes Mount Kosciuszko, which is located in Australia. The reason for this is that Carstensz Pyramid is often closed due to political tensions. The area has had very little Western influence, and there are also tribal issues that are always in play.

Almost immediately after Carstensz, I signed up for Aconcagua in Argentina. I needed to keep climbing to prepare for Everest, as I hadn't done much training in my new role as a "proper" mom. That February, I climbed

Aconcagua. It was incredibly easy for me; I think because I went into the climb with the attitude that it was only a "training climb" for Everest.

On the long walk to the base camp of Aconcagua, the team stopped at a small hut where I had the most amazing steak I'd ever eaten. Covered with salt and perfectly cooked, I saved some to eat on the hike the following day. During the entire Aconcagua trek, I was constantly hungry. The previous group that had summited the mountain hadn't eaten much. Our guides had bought food based on the previous group's appetite, which wasn't enough for us. We were all hungry most of the time, and the guides couldn't believe how much we could eat. (I've had boyfriends say the same thing about me.) Even through the hunger, we had great fun with awesome guides. Except, of course, for that one person… There is always one.

This 22,837-foot goliath of rock and ice is the highest mountain outside of Asia and part of the Principal Cordillera of the Andes. Called the White Sentinel or the Stone Sentinel by ancient indigenous cultures, it's the tallest of many massive peaks. Looking up at it, I wondered whom it was watching. For whom was it standing sentinel? I wondered if it was that one person, the one I was assigned to share my tent with?

She was a bit of a diva, and I was constantly being asked to fill her water bottle and all sorts of other mundane tasks that she could have easily accomplished. She made a lot of money and made damned certain we all knew it. At one point she announced she was diabetic, which she had failed to disclose on the medical forms, and that she controlled her diabetes through diet only.

One morning she woke up with her face swollen to twice its normal size. The guides were terrified of her diabetes. She was allowed to continue, but was watched like a hawk. I offered her my brand-new, purchased-for-Everest goggles because I felt that hers were too tight and too small and might have caused the facial edema.

She ended up summiting but had everyone on edge about her health the entire time. A doctor in the group didn't believe that she was diabetic because at the post-climb dinner she was able to consume a large amount of alcohol without dying. Keeping something that could be life-threatening a secret from the guides, the climbing company, or its clients was dangerous for everyone. Besides being a potential health issue, it might prevent the entire group from reaching the summit if they had to turn back to care for her. I hoped never to be on a climb with her again.

After the summit, we descended to a lower camp on a different side of the mountain. This camp had Coke for sale and I happily forked over six dollars for one can. It was the best six dollars I'd ever spent. The cold bubbles and sugar rush were so needed.

Aconcagua was my sixth completed summit of the seven. While I was climbing Carstensz and Aconcagua, Johnny was on his own Seven Summits mission. He had prevailed over Elbrus in Russia and he, too, had his sights set on Everest.

I felt torn between my children and my passion. Argentina seemed so far away from my kids and Malibu. I knew that Everest would feel even farther away. Todd kept reinforcing that those feelings were normal and that I would feel differently once I was home. I had signed up for Everest, and he didn't want me to back out. I needed to get Everest out of my mind, and the only way to do that was to summit it.

I felt stronger than I ever had to take on what the Nepalese call "Sagarmatha," which means "Goddess of Sky." Custody and support issues were being worked out. I would have full custody of Olivia, and she would continue to live with me full-time once I'd returned from Everest. She was a fifth-grader at Point Dume Marine Science School and was staying with a friend who had two daughters while I was gone. She put up the biggest objection to my scheduled two-month-long Everest climb. I hate to admit it, but I bribed my ten-year-old daughter with a puppy. A woman I know made the snarky comment, "Is she going to call the puppy 'Mom' while you're gone?"

When she complained about my upcoming absence, I told her that in return for two months of her time without me, I would spend the next fifteen years of my time taking care of her dog. That silenced most of the protestations. I had heard of other bribes that had been made so that someone could experience Everest. One of my climbing mates had to buy his wife a pool in order to get the okay from her to climb Everest. I imagine the ranges of bribes that have been made in order to climb this mountain are far more extravagant than a pool or a puppy.

I cringed when I heard things like the "puppy mom" comment, but I knew my lifestyle was very different from most women I knew. A woman leaving her children to climb mountains garnered the instant label of Bad Mom. Thankfully, I had learned to give up the constant desire to please others. With the exception of my children, I didn't care about anyone else's opinion of my life. I finally realized that I wasn't here to live someone else's idea of what my life should be. I only wished they could be as accepting of me as I was of them, even though I didn't always agree with their choices.

Ella was making a great success of her life and, at the age of eighteen, was about to graduate from Simon's Rock, a private college in Massachusetts. Simon's Rock is the sister school to Bard College, and one of two colleges in the country that accepted young people who hadn't graduated from high school but had the intellect and maturity to advance their education. The school was filled with highly intelligent kids who were ready to move on to university courses. Ella had been there for two years and, while her Malibu friends were graduating from Malibu High, she would graduate from Simon's Rock with an AA.

When she left Malibu to attend Simon's Rock back east, the gossip machine went full out. I'd heard the chatter. She was sixteen at that time; why was she leaving home? The stories ranged from her having a baby to her having gone to rehab to any other slanderous scandal they could manufacture. My bright daughter had, in fact, seen the writing on the wall and opted to continue her education instead of all the partying that was going on in Malibu. She wanted more for her future and proved it by heading east for college. Even as a youngster, she was interested in achieving whatever she set her mind to, and I supported her completely, which made it easy for me to smile when I heard the gossip.

My ascent of Everest meant I would miss her graduation, and the guilt I carried was heavier than any pack I'd ever hauled up a mountain. It weighed on my heart. It was tempered only by the knowledge that, right after graduation, she and her boyfriend would fly to Nepal to meet me at base camp. Anticipating that reunion alleviated a bit of the "bad mom" stigma I felt. I knew we would celebrate her graduation and, hopefully, my summit. She was a strong young woman and an excellent hiker, and I knew she could handle the ten-day trek into base camp. In anticipation of her arrival, I wrote little notes to her and left them at the teahouses where I knew she would be staying because Alpine Ascents International (AAI) had arranged her porters and guide along the way.

Johnny was living with my ex and traveling around the world with him to climb mountains. Johnny was determined to reach the achievement of climbing the Seven Summits, and my ex suggested our son was ready to climb Everest. He followed that by saying he'd stop suing me if I agreed to let Johnny ascend that powerful goddess. All I had to do was sign the release for our sixteen-year-old boy to ascend Everest. If I did that, all the pressure and legal maneuvering would end. I felt like I was signing away my son's life in return for the legal issues to stop. Todd assured me that they wouldn't climb Everest that year, especially since they wanted to go up the north side, the Chinese side, of the mountain. I trusted Johnny's ability, his maturity, and his knowledge, so I signed the release, which made him the happiest kid on the planet!

Todd traveled with me to Katmandu and planned to go with me to base camp, stay a few nights, and then head back to Seattle. I was happy for the company and the emotional support. It was refreshing to hear someone say, "You can do this," instead of "You can't do that. You'll never make it." Plus, his insight into the majestic mountain was so helpful. He had made the ascent more than once and had the respect of the guides he employed and the Sherpa.

One morning, while we were lying in bed at the Yak n' Yeti, watching television, Todd suddenly got up and then went right down onto the floor. I thought he might have passed out or had a stroke, and my heart skipped a beat. I had no idea why he was on the floor, but he was rustling around under the bed, so I felt reassured that he was all right. He pulled out something from under the bed. It was a ring, and he asked me to marry him. It was April 1, 2008. I said yes. When we shared the news with a couple of his guides, they thought it was an April Fools' joke.

I had never been happier. I felt light and strong and was engaged to the love of my life. I knew deep down that this would be my year. I didn't have the same stress I had back in 2005. My ex had stopped harassing me with lawsuits, my kids were thriving, and I was engaged. I was ready for Everest.

The trek to base camp from the airport in Lukla takes ten days. Surviving that flight makes you think Everest might be a cakewalk. It's an extremely turbulent, white-knuckle kind of flight, but if you flew straight to base camp from Kathmandu, you could die. The human body has to acclimatize to the lower oxygen levels of high altitude, which is why Lukla is the perfect drop-off spot.

You don't just climb Everest. It's a process of walking and resting, going up and down to get accustomed to the thin air. Just getting to base camp's 17,500-foot elevation can be hard on people. Not everyone reacts to the altitude change in the same way, and some may take longer to feel good with less oxygen filling their lungs.

Once you reach base camp, you get settled in your tent. I immediately organized my tent so that I knew where everything was and could access it in case of an emergency in the middle of the night. Then you take a few days to just rest while you're getting a refresher course about the proper use of various

tools you'll use along the trail. It's always wise to have the refresher course for
fixed line crossings, ladder crossings, ice axes, and crampons.

The days in base camp seemed very long, so to keep my mind and myself
busy, I'd go for daily walks. One of my favorites was to the tent that brought
large ovens with them to make baked goods. The apple pie was to die for.
Showering was another time-killer. I quickly learned that, if you tipped the
porter who brought the bucket of hot water ten or twenty dollars, he'd bring
you an extra bucket. It was worth every penny. Doing laundry was another
way I spent my mornings. You always did laundry in the morning because
if you did it in the afternoon, it might not dry before nightfall, which meant
your clothes would be frozen solid the following morning. The sun beating
down on the tents all day can make the interior feel like an oven but, once the
sun goes down, it's incredibly cold.

While in base camp, we have toilet tents to use. Unlike a lot of the climbers, I
would never leave my tent in the cold and dark of the middle of the night, so I
would use my pee bottle. I only used a yellow bottle for this so it would not be
confused with my drinking bottles. I found that a large-mouth Nalgene bottle
works perfectly—unless you spill it. It takes spilling a huge bottle filled with
urine once to ensure you will never do it again. After that, you carefully screw
the lid back on and make sure it's tight before going back to bed.

During one of my daily walks, I caught myself listening for the voice I heard
while on the Matterhorn, and then again while competing in Race Across
America. It was a voice of warning that alerted me to potential issues. Even
though I was feeling more than capable of summiting Everest, I wondered if
that unidentified inner voice had an opinion.

I had gone with a few friends to climb the Matterhorn in Switzerland. Alpine
Ascents guided it and had a group of clients that ranged from a thirteen-year-
old girl to her father, who was in his fifties. My friends and I were all in our
forties. We had spent a week hiking around the Alps making sure we were fit
enough and acclimatized enough to do the climb. The day before our climb
we hiked up to the Hörnli Hut to get some sleep before the climb. Four a.m.

was the start time for every climber attempting to summit that day, not just Alpine Ascent's group.

We had a full and hearty dinner before crawling into bunk beds that were stacked to the ceiling. I fell asleep easily even though I was a bit nervous. I normally don't like a climb where my whole life depends on someone else not sneezing too hard, or tripping, causing us both to die, and I certainly didn't want to be the reason someone else died.

From a deep sleep, I was awakened by a loud, stern, male voice that was very powerful. It was the kind of voice you don't ignore. It simply said, "No."

I sat up wondering who was talking and waking people in the middle of the night. No one was awake. I knew there was some meaning to it, but I didn't know exactly what that might be. I was unnerved, but somehow realized I'd figure it out when I was meant to. I was avoiding the obvious impact of the voice's statement. I told my rational self—and the voice by proxy—that I would turn around the minute I didn't feel right.

Four a.m. found everyone outside the hut, ready to run as fast as we could to the start of the climb. It is a ridiculous, chaotic scramble among climbers. My guide and I were near the lead. It was pitch-black outside, and the only thing I could see was what was illuminated within the beam of my headlamp. I had told the guide that if I said I was done, I meant it, and I would want to go down immediately. He scoffed at that, but agreed, despite the fact that the Swiss guides pride themselves on how many summits they get.

As morning broke, we were massed together in a human traffic jam. Every so often you could find one bolt to tether yourself to for safety. I was literally attached to the mountain by one inch of the front of my boots and my fingertips. My little group was waiting to clip into the tether with about ten others. People were yelling at each other in various languages and the only word I could pick up was the F-word, which every nationality seemed to know.

The sun rose behind me, and I was able to see how high we were and how precarious my situation was. I was maybe an hour away from the summit. I knew in that moment that this was what the voice was telling me. Even though I had no way of knowing whether anything good or bad was going to happen, I just knew that my time on the mountain was over. I told my guide, "I'm done. Let's head down."

He wasn't happy, but we had an agreement. As we worked our way clear of the pack that was ascending, the thirteen-year-old came up and asked why I was going down. I told her I just wasn't feeling it. She seemed confused by my statement, but I think she also understood.

We returned to the hut, where I got a bottle of champagne and waited for my friends to come down. The Matterhorn was the first time I had not wanted to return to a mountain to finish what I started. There was—and is—zero desire to visit that rocky face again, unlike other mountains I wasn't able to summit.

I don't know if the voice saved me from the Matterhorn, but it felt right that I listened to it, understood its point, and respected it. As I quietly walked around base camp, looking up at the Goddess of the Sky, I listened carefully. The silence made me smile.

Chapter 7

Mt. Everest

Todd stayed at base camp for a few days before returning to Kathmandu. When he departed, I turned my complete attention to the mountain. I was the only woman on a team of men, some of whom I'd climbed with before, but most I had never met. It was a great group, and everyone was looking forward to what we knew could be a treacherous climb.

A few days after arriving in base camp, we had our puja ceremony. No one enters the icefall before this blessing rite. We placed our crampons and ice axes on the altar and had them blessed, along with each of us, for safe passage on the mountain. After such a solemn observance, it seemed odd that shots of Johnny Walker were passed around. I immediately started to feel dizzy. Drinking at altitude is not for the faint of heart.

After a few days, we trekked into the icefall, which sits just above base camp. Timing is everything with that place. The icefall is a constantly moving river of water that's frozen into blocks of ice that can vary in size from a Volkswagen to a small house. And, just as water flows over a waterfall, the ice is always moving down the icefall. You do not want to be under or on top of a chunk of ice when it moves. If you happen to be in the wrong place at the wrong time, your body will probably never be recovered from under the tons of ice.

There are numerous ladder crossings in the icefall. Some of the crevasses are so deep all you see is black when you look down under your feet. Trying to navigate a slippery ladder with crampons is hard enough, but when you look down into an abyss of nothingness, your heart beats a little faster. I always made certain that I clipped into the ropes that I'd use as handrails across the ladder. It's easy to get lazy or anxious, not take the time to clip into the ropes, and just try to hurry across. One gust of wind could knock you off, or the ladder could move unexpectedly and you would tumble into a deep chasm.

Once the team had acclimatized and was feeling strong, we hiked to Camp One, which is part of our rotations up the mountain. We spent the night and returned to base camp the following morning. A few days later we returned to Camp One to spend the night. The next day we hiked up to Camp Two, where we stayed for a few days at an elevation of 21,300 feet before returning down the mountain to base camp. The idea of this type of acclimatization is to gradually expose the body to higher elevations before returning to lower altitudes to recuperate and rest. Going up and down the mountain goes on for weeks because it's important that climbers' bodies have enough time to adapt to the decrease in oxygen. Failure to acclimate correctly can lead to acute mountain sickness, high-altitude pulmonary edema (HAPE), or high-altitude cerebral edema (HACE). That's why climbers have the saying, "Climb high and sleep low."

We spent weeks going up and down the mountain in preparation for our summit attempt. In the icefall, I could hear big cracking sounds. You instinctively freeze for a second like a mouse in a mousetrap, and then look around quickly to see what is falling and from where. Because the rocks and avalanches usually started falling thousands of feet above us, we had time to move out of the way. I realized the acclimatization process was about more than oxygen; it was also about mentally preparing you to be alert to the natural hazards on the mountain. You hear something and you quickly process the direction and the danger quotient before going farther.

There are two ways to get from Camp One to Camp Two, depending on the ice. You might need to walk up and down through more seracs or ridges of ice, where it's necessary to clip in and out a hundred times, or you might walk as a rope team on the edges of the ice, just below Nuptse. We were able to walk on the side, which was a blessing, as it was much faster. The biggest potential problem we faced was rockfall. The noise from a rockslide sounded like a jet engine, but we knew it was a small piece of mountain beginning its descent far above us. It was nerve-wracking because there was a constant barrage of rocks falling from above that made climbing near the base of Nuptse a life-and-death maneuver to stay out of the line of fire.

An issue that I specifically had was that, while I felt physically at the top of my game, I couldn't help but feel I was suffocating every time I put an oxygen mask on. I ripped the mask off to try to catch my breath because I felt I couldn't breathe, which is the exact opposite of what it was actually doing.

At one point, just as we were leaving Camp Three, the guide said, "If you take that mask off again, you're going back down."

I had to learn to trust that the big mask that covered my face was not going to kill me. I kept reminding myself that it was like scuba diving; I had to relax and keep my breathing slow and steady. I also didn't want to blow through all of my oxygen. I wanted to be able to conserve as much O2 as possible so I could turn the air to high while I was above Camp Four. Besides the obvious benefit of oxygen, it gave me quite the appetite and helped keep me warm.

As I approached Camp Three on one of our acclimatization rounds, I knew we weren't going any higher than that, and were simply giving our bodies a chance to adjust to the elevation before going back down. I was navigating the steep slope of the Lhotse Face, when someone in our area announced that a person from the AAI office back in Seattle had called to say that Ella had just been accepted to NYU. She had called them to get the message to me and I was ecstatic! I felt good at that altitude, felt great on the climb up, and to be greeted with this amazing news was an incredible high. I made many satellite phone calls while I was climbing Everest, but this one was special. She had received acceptances from numerous universities but had hoped for—and gotten—admission to NYU. I was thrilled for her!

The rigorous routing of acclimatization ends with a night at Camp Three, which is perched on the side of the Lhotse Face. After that, we walked all the way back down to the valley where trees and plants grow. Oxygen at that level helped to heal any wounds we might have incurred over the past three to five weeks. Wounds are hard to heal in the oxygen-poor environment of base camp and higher. Mouth sores are common from constantly sucking on hard candy to keep your mouth moist in the dry air. And, while back in greenery, appetites return. When we are down in the valley, we're encouraged to eat as much as we want as many times a day as possible. Whatever weight is gained will be lost going back up the mountain.

The men on my team had to wear belts to keep their pants up because they'd lost so much weight. I, on the other hand, didn't lose a pound. I never lost my appetite. Maybe that's why I felt so good the whole time—I never let my fuel run low. I was, however, incredulous that my pants were getting tight when all of my teammate's pants were falling off. I felt it was a serious injustice.

We had stopped on the Lhotse Face for a water break on our way down from Camp Three during a round of acclimatization. A French couple met us on their way up and were quite upset that people had thrown things at them from above. I had no idea what they were talking about until I realized that my pee funnel had slipped on the slick ice and made a straight line for them as they were coming up. The bummer was I really needed that funnel when we climbed to higher elevations.

When you're female, in your harness and clipped into a rope, it's impossible to pee with a snowsuit on. A pee funnel allows you to urinate standing up. It requires unzipping a zipper, not undoing your entire harness and half your suit. My amazing Sherpa, Chewang, who has since passed away, made a new one for me out of a discarded plastic soda bottle we found on the South Col. That ingenious solution worked far better than my store-bought funnel.

Weather forecasters based in Switzerland and Seattle helped make the climbing decision for us. They predicted decent weather for the coming week, and we finally had the go-ahead for our summit attempt. The Sherpa thought this was too much technology. They just stuck their heads out of the dining tent to see if it was safe to climb. As they saw it, the Sherpa knowledge of the Goddess of the Sky, her winds and storms and numerous characteristics, couldn't be matched by any technology. They know—and understand—how her heart beats.

We left the following morning for Camp Two. By this time, our team was fast enough to go straight to Camp Two, bypassing Camp One. The Sherpa don't like to sleep at Camps One or Three. They don't think it's safe. In my travels, I'd encountered several indigenous people who avoided anything that had to do with odd numbers. I didn't know if it was superstition or understanding the heartbeat of the mountain.

We spent one night at Camp Two and, the following day, headed to Camp Three on the Lhotse Face. Upon arrival, we started chipping away at the ice to make a platform large enough to place a tent. You must be careful anywhere you walk on the Lhotse Face because it is literally the steep face of the mountain covered in slick ice. If you fall, you are not going to stop anytime soon. It is almost always a certain death. Once the platforms were built, we moved into our tents, where I snacked on spicy wasabi peas. My tent mate, John Soebing, made me laugh at something and a pea got stuck. I was choking, started coughing, and couldn't catch my breath. Panic set in. Caught in the mental fear of suffocation, I tried telling myself that I was surrounded by air. I knew I was lying to myself, but I thought it would help. I kept thinking, *Just calm down*. I couldn't. Choking while at Camp Three, at 24,500 feet elevation, is not like choking at sea level. I was immediately out of breath and panicking. I clawed at the sides of the tent the way a drowning person claws at their rescuer. John called Vern Tejas, a world-renowned mountaineer and one of our guides, over to help. Another climber, Mark, grabbed me from behind to try to calm my breathing while Vern made me try to match his breaths in an effort to slow my breathing.

Vern made a joke about my sat (blood oxygen saturation) level being in the forties. "If we were anywhere else on the planet, you'd be in an ICU." Here on Everest, it was just another day. While this was happening, we heard a small explosion, and Jose Luis Peralvo, our Ecuadorian guide, screamed. One of the cookstove fuel bottles had exploded. *Great*, I thought, *I'm suffocating, and someone just blew themselves up next door*. I realized it could be Jose Luis and thought, *Oh no! Our guide is dead*. Finally, after thirty minutes of trying to slow and calm my breathing, I caught my breath. Thankfully, Jose Luis was unhurt. I vowed to never climb with wasabi pea snacks again.

After a night at Camp Three, we made our way up the steep Lhotse Face and across the yellow band of rock that separates Everest from Lhotse. A man was coming down, being short-roped by a guide. His eyes were bandaged shut. He was suffering from snow blindness, an excruciatingly painful thing to experience. I made a mental note to myself to never remove my goggles for summit photos.

An hour or so later, there it was, the elusive and invisible Camp Four, otherwise known as the South Col. It was a place I had read about and imagined for years, and it was finally in front of me. We found our tents that the Sherpa had set up for us and got settled in. Vern was my tent mate. I tried to play Sudoku, the numbers game that I had been playing in all of the camps. I used it to evaluate how my brain was working. At the South Col, I couldn't even finish the most basic puzzles. I felt fine, but my brain was not functioning as well as I thought it was.

Our team was given the nine p.m. time slot to leave the following night. My appetite had never left, so I ate a huge dinner and felt great. While squatting in my tent to pee into my little bottle, I again noticed my thighs looked huge. *What the hell,* I said to myself. *How is it possible that everyone else is losing so much weight and I haven't lost a pound?* Then I berated myself for being an idiot, worrying about the size of my thighs while on the South Col. I reminded myself of two things: A) *No one else is up here worrying about the size of their thighs,* and B) *These thighs helped get me up here, so stop whining and get into your snowsuit.*

The crowds of people slowed us down a bit along the south summit. There was a long line of people on one rope and passing someone had to be done with extreme care. If you weren't properly clipped in and you fell, you were not going to survive the fall. When we reached the Balcony, a small platform where we could rest for a moment, I could no longer feel my feet. All I felt were large stumps at the end of my legs. We were 27,600 feet up the frozen mountain and I couldn't feel my feet.

Lakpa Rita Sherpa made me stop after I said I couldn't feel them. Summit fever had me in its grip. I had to summit and I didn't care if I lost any toes at that point. I actually thought toes were a small price to pay for summiting Everest. Lakpa Rita Sherpa took his last pair of socks out of his backpack and put them on my feet. My feet stayed warm the rest of the climb, and I truly believe his actions are the only reason I still have all my toes.

I waited my turn at the Hilary Step, which is a nearly vertical chunk of rock. It requires traversing narrow, steep ridges while navigating treacherous rock and ice formations. You have to use your ascender to clip into the ropes, some of which were merely frozen in place and might or might not have been attached to the mountain. You never knew for certain. When it was my turn to clip in, I grabbed the newest-looking rope I could, attached my ascender to it, and prayed that I had clipped into a new, still-attached-to-the-mountain length of rope. For good measure, I grabbed a handful of other ropes with my free hand as I slid my ascender up. Thirty feet later I was up the Hilary Step. The summit was much closer now, and I knew that, no matter what, I would stand on the pinnacle of Mount Everest.

Seven weeks after arriving in Nepal, at seven a.m. Nepal time, May 24, 2008, my friend and guide, Chewang, and I stood feet from my goal. After debating who should go first, with each telling the other to "Please, go ahead," we walked arm in arm the last few feet to the summit. I had climbed the Seven Summits, a feat that fewer than thirty women had achieved at that time. It had been a grueling ten-hour climb, but any thought of discomfort vanished with the reality that I was standing atop my seventh of the Seven Summits. I had always pictured myself standing there crying. I thought my tears would come from the achievement, the beauty, and the personal success I felt. But the tears weren't there. I wanted to cry, but all I could feel was gratitude to God for allowing me to be in this place. It was a heartfelt, spiritual moment in which I felt surrounded by Creation, as if this were the home of God. I surveyed the amazing panorama and silently said the Lord's Prayer. Then I felt an overwhelming need to call my kids.

Instead of my usual custom of calling all of the kids when I reached a summit, I called my close friend, Kelly Chapman Meyer, from the top. I had loaned my personal satellite phone to a teammate while we were at Camp Three. While it was in his tent, he had spilled a hot cup of tea on it, which rendered it useless. Once on the summit, I begged another climber from another team if I could borrow his phone to make a quick call. Thankfully, he agreed.

I had called Kelly ten hours earlier, right before we started the ascent. I told her to expect another call from me in about thirteen hours. She agreed that she would call each of my children to let them know I had safely reached the summit of Mount Everest.

The call from the summit was physically painful, as it was thirty degrees below zero and I had to take my heavy gloves and oxygen mask off to dial and speak. My glove liners did not offer much protection in the frigid air. Kelly answered on the first ring and was screaming congratulations. She immediately promised to call the kids for me. Her enthusiasm came right through the phone, but I could no longer feel my hand or face. I had to hang up and knew she would understand.

After the call, I bent over to pick up some rocks to take home to mark the occasion. I didn't realize how top heavy I was with the oxygen tanks in my pack. I started to fall forward toward Camp Two, thousands of feet below. Panicked, I threw myself backward, frozen with fear and adrenaline. I had almost fallen off the summit of Everest. It took a moment to calm down, but I was steady when the rest of the team arrived on top. After a few pictures and congratulatory hugs, Chewang and I left. We had been on the summit for an hour.

I had remembered the lesson I'd learned about climbing too fast. My ascent had been steady and at a relatively slow pace for me. The descent was different. Chewang and I ran down every part of the mountain that we could. I was hyper from the thrill of summiting and Chewang is Sherpa, so running down Everest was nothing for him. About forty-five minutes or so from our tents on the South Col, we came upon the well-known climber, Kenton Cool, who was sitting next to a corpse whose face was covered, but the rest of whose body, in its snowsuit, was still visible. I had seen the corpse the night before on my way to the summit. Not wanting to be disrespectful of the individual who had passed, I kept my head down and followed the glow of my headlamp. I tried to remain focused on what I needed to do, knowing there was nothing I could do for that person. I had never seen a dead body just lying around. It felt surreal, like seeing a hippo on the jungle cruise ride at Disneyland. It was there, but not real.

"What's up, Kenton?" I asked.
"Dianette, it's Rob," he said.

Rob Milne had been to Everest with me in 2005 and had summited Mount Vinson with me in Antarctica in 2003. When going through the icefall, he had been capable of having a perfect conversation while I would be huffing and puffing trying to catch my breath. He was incredibly fit and strong. For whatever reason, and I don't know if he was going up or down, he bent over his ice axe and collapsed.

Kenton had been with him when it happened and had tried to save him. I gently suggested that it was time that we all get up and get moving and that we would toast Rob back in the safety of Kathmandu. Sitting around anywhere in the death zone on Everest was not a good idea. Kenton nodded in agreement.

As an additional reminder of the danger involved in climbing, an avalanche cut loose as we were on our way down through the icefall. We could hear it as it started, which gave us enough time to look up and around to see where it originated. That's why you never wear headphones while climbing; you have to be able to hear what's happening around and, more importantly, above you. I moved to stand behind a man whose larger frame shielded me from the blow back of ice as it frosted him.

Chewang and I continued our run to our tents. By ten thirty in the morning, I was back in my warm sleeping bag and thinking of Rob. If someone as fit and experienced as he was could die on a mountain, what business did I—the mother of three children—have being up there in the death zone? The guilt I felt was heavy and, as usual, I promised myself that I was done. But this time was different. I meant it this time and went so far as to give all of my climbing gear away once I was back down at base camp, including my specially made navy blue Feathered Friends down suit that had extra fill to keep me warm. I was very serious this time about giving up all extreme sports.

Around noon, Vern and the rest of the team returned to their tents on the South Col. All had summited. As Vern climbed into our tent he asked simply, "Everest or Fiji?" We both laughed as I said, "Fiji! 100 percent Fiji!" We had both done Eco-Challenge Fiji in 2002 and agreed that it was far more difficult than climbing Everest.

I was looking forward to meeting up with Ella. We had a lot to celebrate. Her graduation and acceptance to NYU, even though she eventually chose Barnard, and my official conquering of the Seven Summits on the Carstensz Pyramid list. The monkey of Everest was finally off my back.

After a huge celebration back in base camp, I packed what little gear I had left and, the following day, headed back down the valley to Pheriche where I, along with a few of the other climbers, could hopefully catch a helicopter back to Kathmandu.

I put my duffel bag into my room and headed to the sunroom to read. As I was lying on my back, book above my head, a young woman walked into the sunroom and said, "Hi."

She said it as though she knew me. I apologized and asked if we had met. She took off her bucket hat and said, "Mom!"

I was shocked! She had made it! The porters had told me over the radio that she was much farther down the valley and I thought I would miss seeing her before I flew back to Kathmandu. I jumped up and hugged her. She looked so little and so young. My mind was probably in a haze from the climb, but I hadn't recognized my own child. She and her boyfriend and I had a great time together. They watched the next day as I boarded the helicopter to Kathmandu while they continued on to base camp to see the sprawling tent city and the icefall.

I returned home from Mount Everest on May 28, 2008. I had full custody of Olivia, and I told her that with our upcoming move to Bainbridge Island,

I was done with extreme sports. The move wasn't what we had hoped for. Todd and I were able to see each other more, but Olivia was the new kid at school and missed her friends, and I learned something about myself. While Bainbridge is beautiful and I loved being so close to Seattle, I desperately missed the long hiking hill that leads to Buzzard's Roost in Malibu. There was nothing like that for me on the island. I had no way of getting that workout without driving an hour. I had big hills and an amazing trail system in Malibu, and it was proving impossible to replicate that with anything on Bainbridge. My soul and my head needed that hill. I had always believed that I could live anywhere. As long as I had my kids and a decent home, I could be happy. Not true. I need big hills with a good trail or two. We moved back where we could both be content.

Todd and I tried to make it work after I returned to Malibu, but the distance was too great, and I had Olivia full-time. There was no more week-on, week-off schedule with my ex, so flying to see Todd every other week was not going to happen. I did get back into my routine, trained for little events here and there, and still climbed a little in the summertime, but mostly I was home raising Olivia.

I knew Johnny and his dad were scheduled to climb Everest that same year, but they planned to go up the north side, which was controlled by the Chinese. I was terrified and furious over that decision. I had faith that my sixteen-year-old son was talented and knowledgeable, but I didn't think he was ready for the north side. If something happened, it would be harder to address a rescue, as it's more exposed and more difficult to get someone down from the top if there were to be a problem. Todd had told me that they wouldn't go to Everest that year, and he was right. The Chinese government closed the north side to climbers because they wanted to get the Olympic torch to the summit without any interference. Since Everest was out, Johnny and my ex decided to set their sights on Denali and Aconcagua, both of which they succeeded at summiting. Everest would have to wait another year for Johnny, and I could breathe a little easier.

Chapter 8

Johnny, doing a back flip. North Pole.
(Filmed by a Russian with a Go-Pro.)

E verest had waited for seventeen-year-old Johnny. The additional year to train and grow bigger and stronger had served him well. Physically, he was a beast and had developed a remarkably mature mental attitude. Todd and I flew to Nepal to meet Johnny and his dad on their way to base camp. I was happy that they were now climbing on the south side. We wanted to wish the father and son duo luck on their climb. As we talked, I shared the best advice I'd received pertaining to summiting that magnificent mountain: "Everest is the same rock, snow, and ice you've always climbed on. There's no difference." Jeanne Stawiecki had told me that and it always stayed with me. It was so true. It's a bit higher and more expensive, but all of us mountaineers have walked on similar terrain for years. You can't let the name freak you out.

One thing that I'd noticed was that most of those who quit didn't seem to get past Camp Three. I suspected that was because you can't see Camp Four until you are right on top of it. I told Johnny and his dad to just trust that it is there and that, when they picked up rocks from the summit, they should bend at the knees. Don't take a chance of falling off the mountain like I almost had. I was nervous and excited for Johnny to finally have a go at climbing Mount Everest.

On May 26, 2009, Johnny set the world record as the youngest person to climb the Seven Summits.

I was over the moon! But I also knew that there would always be another mountain, another summit, and another big wave. He did a string of publicity interviews, but never rested on his accomplishments. He was always pushing the envelope with some extreme sport.

While driving to a doctor's appointment for Johnny and Olivia, I noticed numerous news vans parked on the side of the Pacific Coast Highway. "Wow, must be a lot of whales out of season," I said to the kids.

Johnny sunk down in the seat. With a spunky, crooked grin that I knew too well, he said, "Those might be for me."

Considering all the publicity he'd recently received, I told him to stop being so conceited. When we got home, I turned on the television, only to hear, "Malibu teen caught car surfing. News at six."

"Johnny!" I screamed. "We're going to watch this together." That was followed by, "What were you thinking?"

We watched the news as we ate. I called his girlfriend and asked her to join us for dinner, and I cooked Johnny's favorite meal. He received less than favorable publicity with that stunt. He'd been photographed "car surfing" on top of a moving automobile on the Pacific Coast Highway and the images were all over the six o'clock news. I couldn't help but notice that he wasn't "surfing," he was "flying"—chest out, arms spread wide, and leaning into the wind. It was the exact position he had struck on the bow of the boat at age ten and while paragliding at age nine. At seventeen, he was still searching for the freeing feeling of flight.

His father and I were not impressed with this stunt. We asked him to apologize publicly, which he did through a video he posted online. When it was time to see the judge, I was with Johnny at the Malibu Courthouse. I was shocked that there was no hearing, just a window where I paid a small fine. In true Johnny fashion, the young woman behind the counter was all smiles while she spoke with Johnny. I told her to stop encouraging him; Johnny could charm anyone. Much later, I heard from a few moms that he had done this stunt numerous times speeding through the canyons at night. He just liked the feeling of flying on top of a car. He never filmed those escapades. There were so many things he did that, thankfully, I knew nothing about.

I was settled into a routine with Olivia at home. While I wasn't climbing big mountains or doing expedition-length races, I was training and doing some smaller events here and there. I enjoyed being outside and being a mom. Even though I wasn't tackling any serious sport, I was still having fun.

Some things I had anticipated being fun were quite the opposite. My friend's husband, Leslie, had invited me to jet-ski with him from Marina Del Rey to the island of Catalina, located thirty-eight nautical miles off the coast of Southern California. That had been on my bucket list for years, so I of course said yes. It was a really foggy morning, which let Leslie and me kill some time at a local coffee house. When the fog had cleared a bit, he said it was time to go. We got onto two jet skis and headed to the Palos Verdes peninsula, where we could make a direct line to the island. We agreed that when we got halfway across, if we couldn't see the island, we would turn around, and return to the marina.

Halfway across, the fog was thick around the island. We sat on our skis to assess the situation, and decided the only thing to do was to return. In the short amount of time that it had taken us to make that call, dense fog had completely enveloped us. We couldn't see more than a hundred feet in any direction. Stupidly, neither of us had brought a compass. We had no idea what direction we were facing. Leslie started to go in the direction he thought was east, headed for shore. As far as I could tell we might have been headed for Mexico, Alaska, or Hawaii. We were going full-throttle toward something we couldn't see, with zero idea where we truly headed.

Suddenly, I was hit by a swell that knocked me off and away from my jet ski. Even though I was wearing the bracelet that stops the engine in case you fall off, it didn't stop the jet ski's forward motion. I tried swimming as fast as I could toward it, but the current was taking the machine farther and farther away from me, at a much faster pace than I could swim. I felt the vastness of the open ocean, in the middle of a shipping lane, heavy with sharks, and shrouded in fog. I stopped trying to swim and curled up into a little ball, hoping that by staying still, I wouldn't attract any sharks. I was completely screwed and I knew it. My safety check-in call that I had pre-arranged with Olivia wasn't for four more hours. My phone was in the front of the jet ski in the waterproof compartment. I wondered where they would find my body, or even if they would find it. I also wondered what would kill me: would it be a ship or a shark? *You complete idiot*, I said to myself over and over. I kept my legs pulled in tight to my chest to avoid dangling them like shark bait. One of my worst fears in life was playing out for real.

After ten minutes or so, which felt like eternity, Leslie showed up on his ski. He had turned around at some point realizing that I was nowhere near him. I raised my arms and screamed, "Leslie, get me out of this water!"

His response upon seeing me flailing in the water, yelling, was, "I didn't think you'd act like this in the water."

Was he kidding me? How should one act in this situation? I was pissed when I climbed onto his machine but I didn't say anything. We drove around for a while until we found my ski. My ski was much slower than his, which was why I couldn't keep up, but now I was afraid to go too fast in case I was hit by another swell. As the fog started to clear a little, the lighthouse on the peninsula became visible. We turned slightly left and started to see the ships that were docked outside of the marina to unload.

We entered the safety of the marina, and an hour or so later, I had one of the biggest adrenaline rushes I had ever had. I didn't even know what that feeling was, but I didn't like it. I was super-wired and ecstatic to be alive. I vowed to never put myself into a position like that again, never to allow my life to fully be in someone else's hands. I scolded myself: *I should have had my cell phone on my person and I should have had a compass as well.* I knew I needed to be responsible for myself in the outdoors, no matter how competent those around may be.

———

Johnny was unstoppable. He turned eighteen in December, and in January began skydiving certification lessons in Perris, California. He was learning the accelerated free fall (AFF) method and loved it. He was so dedicated to AFF that within the month of January he had progressed through all seven levels of training and received his solo jump certification.

Skydiving was his passion. He jumped from balloons and planes and anything that had height. He was getting quite the reputation and was invited to attend the National University of Singapore's "What makes a Young Champion" event in August, where he was awarded the honor of "Youth Champion"

at the 2010 inaugural Olympic Youth Games. We expected him to enroll at
the University of Southern California once he returned from Singapore, but
he had other ideas. He decided to push college back a semester and move
to Las Vegas to further his skydiving skills and train with Matt Rosado, a
professional skydiver.

On a trip to Twin Falls, Idaho, Matt taught Johnny how to BASE jump.
BASE is an acronym that stands for building, antenna, span, and earth. The
letters represent the four primary "exit points" that BASE jumpers leap from,
including buildings, antennas, bridges, and cliffs. Even though a parachute
is used to land safely, it is considered an extreme sport that adds an extra
dimension to skydiving, which makes it more dangerous.

I remembered back to a time when Olivia had sent me a text saying, "Johnny
hit a mountain."

I pulled off the highway, into a Taco Bell parking lot, and nervously called
Johnny's cell. He answered, and I could feel the tension leaving my body. He
explained that he had hit a mountain while paragliding and had broken his
tailbone. To him it was nothing serious, but I knew the pain he would be in
and hoped and prayed he would learn from it. It wasn't the first time he'd
escaped death, which had become par for the course. He had cheated death
so many times that I just assumed that would always be the case—close to the
line, but never crossing it.

Leaping from the Perrine Bridge, which stands four hundred eighty-six feet
above the Snake River, Johnny once again embraced the feeling of flight. The
Perrine Bridge is considered the safest legal BASE jump in the US.

The Grand Canyon is not considered safe or legal because BASE jumping is
prohibited in all national parks. When Johnny called to tell me that he and his
friends were going to the Grand Canyon to BASE jump, I was initially relaxed
about it. I knew he was capable. He told me not to expect any phone calls
from him because they wouldn't have service, and it might be a couple of days
before we could talk again.

On September 20, less than a month after jumping from the Perrine Bridge, Johnny and three of his friends and mentors leapt from a towering cliff into the Grand Canyon.

On the second morning of his trip, I woke at three in the morning, restless and feeling furious about something, but I didn't know what. I only knew it had something to do with Johnny. I climbed out of bed, made my way to the living room, and fell onto the couch, where I spent most of the day staring blankly at a silent television. I was mad and, yet, not sure what I was mad about. I just knew that I had no control over the situation. I couldn't reach him, and I hadn't heard from him. Then, finally, he called.

The jump was fine and exhilarating, but he and his friends had almost died after they completed the jump. They were relying on old maps and thought there would be a trail back up from the canyon floor near the spot where they'd landed. They searched, but the trail was nowhere to be found. For two days they'd wandered the canyon's floor, without water or food, looking for a way out.

The temperatures at night were so cold they wrapped themselves in their parachutes to stay warm, and during the day the heat was unbearable. Johnny resorted to drinking his own urine because they had no water. Finally, one of them found some rope hanging from the cliff's edge. He climbed it and got help.

When Johnny climbed out of the canyon, he was wearing only his underwear and tennis shoes because of the intense heat. There were plenty of police waiting for them at the top of the rim, as they were trespassing on tribal lands. A rescue helicopter arrived as the men slugged down water and answered questions from tribal police. Fortunately, the police felt sorry for them, and said they had suffered enough. They let them go without citing or arresting the BASE jumpers.

I never really considered anything Johnny did as legal or illegal because, by the time I knew about most of his adventures, he was home safe and sound. A lot of BASE jumpers do illegal jumps and, when they're caught, their chutes are confiscated and they have to pay fines. Johnny somehow managed to avoid that.

Once more, Johnny had survived and come home. He told me that one of the thoughts that horrified him during this ordeal was of his dad and me finding out that he had died. Still, that horrifying thought wasn't enough to stop him from furthering his jumping pursuits. I understood. I can't explain the kind of hold adventure sports can have over you; I can't even fully explain it to myself. It's an addiction. Yes, it's the rush, the danger, and the challenge of pushing and testing your limits, and yourself, both mentally and physically. Once it's in your soul, it never leaves. I couldn't fault Johnny for following his dreams and his heart when I had done the same.

The four friends' ability to survive at the bottom of the Grand Canyon earned them a starring role on Bear Grylls's *Escape from Hell*. Soon after, he signed a contract with his first sponsor. Sponsors are hard to come by when the adventures are so extreme. They usually have to be related to the particular sport or race, but Johnny's was an energy drink, which I thought was quite appropriate.

In November, he announced that he intended to skydive onto the North Pole. He'd already completed the Seven Summits and been to the South Pole. Reaching the North Pole at his age would make him the youngest to complete the "Explorer's Grand Slam." This is one of the most coveted adventure achievements, and fewer than one hundred people have successfully accomplished all three.

When he told me of his plans, I was terrified. Several years earlier, there had been a group that attempted to skydive onto the South Pole. Of the four, one survived. Parachutes had opened partially or not at all, and the single survivor said he was surrounded by white, blinded by the sun, with no point of reference. Had the chutes frozen? Was it equipment malfunction? What caused this horrific tragedy? Would it be the same at the North Pole? What if the chutes didn't open because they froze, or were somehow affected by the extreme temperatures? I wished I had more control of the situation.

Then I thought back to times when I did things and I was certain my children wished they controlled me. I recognized some of what I had probably put my children through and quietly thanked them from the bottom of my heart for letting me experience my adventures and for letting me be me. I realized on a deeper level than I ever had before, that nothing can—or should be— controlled by another. I had to accept my son for who and what he was, and that included the daredevil side of him that I genuinely appreciated.

I knew I couldn't stop Johnny from attempting his goal, so I reached out to Todd and asked that he help with logistics. Todd made the necessary calls and assured me that every safety measure was in place. The company that was handling the logistics and safety measures had arranged for Johnny to jump with two Russian military men, just in case anything went wrong. I appreciated the effort, and it did ease my apprehension a little. I was still a mother, though, and the day of his jump I was sick with worry.

I knew the exact time of his jump, and planned my morning around it because I knew I'd need distractions. As I drove down the Pacific Coast Highway just south of Pepperdine University, it occurred to me, *For the next hour, I am the mother of a son. I have a son.* I wondered what would happen if in an hour I wasn't and didn't?

I arrived at Marmalade Café in Malibu and told my companion why my cell would be on the table—face up—as we ate, which was something I never did. When my phone rang halfway through breakfast, my heart skipped a beat. I hurried to answer it, and when I heard Johnny on the other end, I was ecstatic. He had pulled off quite the feat and had succeeded in achieving the Explorer's Grand Slam! I was so happy for him, and equally relieved.

When he shared the video footage of the events, I was proud of him. I watched the helicopter land to pick them up and then roll out two dainty, tiny steps for the Russians and my son to climb onboard. Those delicate little steps seemed the antithesis of what the three men had just accomplished. I couldn't help but laugh and say out loud, "After a jump like that—just take a big step into the helicopter!"

Chapter 9

Mt. Timpanogos, Utah

The University of Southern California saw something in Johnny that wasn't reflected in grades and test scores. In return, Johnny was loyal to USC and to his fraternity, Sigma Chi. When he landed at the North Pole, he pulled out banners for both. USC provided an amazing college experience and Sigma Chi brought trusted friendships to his life. It also introduced him to the love of his life, Piper Gates.

With Ella rooted in her studies in New York at Barnard, and Johnny at USC and pursuing his sports at every opportunity, I was at home with Olivia. She was my primary focus. The only one of my children who actually attended high school full-time, all the way through, Olivia embraced the whole high school experience. She and I shared several trips and tame adventures that replaced most of my climbing and racing trips. Raising teenagers was far more time-consuming and involved than little ones. I heard one mom refer to mountaineering and say, "Oh, I'll do that when the kids are a bit older." My thought was, no you won't. That's when they need you the most and you really need to be home. Teenagers are no joke.

Olivia and I were on a spring break vacation when she excitedly said, "Look at this, Mom!" She showed me a video of someone big-wave surfing in Hawaii.

"That's nice," I said, not really paying attention to the image on the screen.

"It's Johnny," she squealed.

Johnny was also on spring break with some friends on the North Shore of Oahu where he was introduced to a man named Garrett McNamara. Johnny managed to convince Garrett to tow him into the big waves. Garrett thought the kid was nuts, but after getting approval from my former racing teammate, Mike Trisler, who happened to be nearby, Garrett agreed. My son could talk people into the craziest things, and he did it with confidence and that beautiful smile.

A few years later, when Johnny was twenty-one, I was sitting at a USC football game when Garrett called me to ask permission to take Johnny to Nazare,

Portugal, to surf. Johnny was a legal adult, with no need for anyone to ask my permission for anything. I always thought it was incredibly kind of Garrett to do that. I told him he had better bring my son home in one piece, and he said he would do his best.

Johnny rode a forty-foot wave while in Portugal and loved it. Big wave surfing is the one thing I can absolutely guarantee I will never do. I am terrified of big waves and, basically, of the ocean in general. Johnny came home safe and happy. He'd had another big adventure and returned unscathed, but it still wasn't enough for him. He was committed to training to be a Navy SEAL, going to USC, and primarily his love of skydiving and BASE jumping.

Johnny had a bit of a double standard. He always told me that I had no ground to stand on when lecturing him about his sports since I, a mother of three, had climbed Everest. "Mothers should not climb Everest," he would admonish.

I used to wonder how many people felt sorry for the children of a mom who took time to participate in extreme sports. They enjoyed their dinner parties, weekend getaways, and other adult activities that didn't include their kids. Somehow that was okay and different from a mom who raced and climbed mountains. I know that some felt I set a poor example for my kids, but I felt I was instilling a sense of independence, adventure, and self-reliance. I knew all three of my children were quite capable of taking care of themselves. I used to joke with them that I could drop them off anywhere in the world and they would have no problem figuring out how to get home. My mom had instilled in me a "take care of yourself" attitude, and I wanted my kids to have the same confidence.

I remember one mom referred to Johnny's wild side (at the age of two) by saying, "Thank God he isn't my son!" While she and others couldn't understand why I didn't forbid some of the things my children did, I loved their desire to explore and push their physical limitations and boundaries. I appreciated the fact that they studied, learned, and trained before they attempted something new. They weighed the risk-advantage matrix and were usually quite smart about their decisions. I had learned to trust my instincts and myself, and I was learning to trust their talent, ability, and ingenuity.

Despite Johnny's declaration that moms shouldn't climb Everest, I looked at my sports the same way Johnny viewed his; the reward was always worth the risk, and the risk was always acceptable and not so big that the sport was worth giving up. I was rarely afraid while climbing or racing, and I hardly ever felt that I was risking my life. I always felt safe, and I trusted my instinct to turn around if I wasn't feeling comfortable or I was afraid. I had turned around on mountains a few times, with no regret, when something seemed off. I had shared my perspective with him and hoped that he would also rely on that inner knowing.

Johnny honed in on wingsuit BASE jumping. His former pursuits of big wave surfing, downhill and longboard skateboarding, and high-altitude mountaineering took a back seat. He had successfully reached the pinnacle of everything he'd attempted. Before he could pursue his first wingsuit BASE jump, he knew that he had to be an expert in both skydiving and BASE jumping, amass as many jumps as possible, and log hours of practice time flying his wingsuit. Determined to succeed, he took every opportunity to make the one-and-a-half-hour drive to skydive in Perris while he attended classes at USC.

Not all of Johnny's jumps were serious training. He made YouTube videos of his aerial shenanigans which included illegally BASE jumping from an antenna that he labeled "Nunyobznes" tower in Africa, to landing on a golf course, to executing a triple corkscrew flip out of a hot-air balloon. His comfort and confidence in the air was undeniable. By the end of the semester, Johnny was regularly flying in his wingsuit, leaping from both airplanes and hot-air balloons, and his count of jumps reached triple digits.

I couldn't say much about Johnny's adventures, as I was still feeding my addiction with smaller events. While Olivia was in middle school and high school, I managed to climb Mount Whitney seven more times, Mount Kilimanjaro three more times, the Matterhorn, Mount Khuiten, Mount

Blanc, and a few peaks in Ecuador; trek to Everest base camp; participate in ultras; and do the Gobi March and the Atacama Crossing. I summited Mount Rainier, did the Rim to Rim to Rim run in the Grand Canyon, the Las Vegas Challenge, Cactus to Clouds, the Avalon 50, and the Million Dollar Challenge. I also spent time scuba diving with Olivia. Even though I loved being a mom and flipping houses, I couldn't quite give up my adventurous side.

Neither could Johnny. Over summer break from school, he headed to Switzerland, where he planned his first wingsuit BASE jump. He selected Kandersteg, a hotspot for the sport, that's located in a picturesque river valley in the Bernese Alps. He had learned how to analyze a jump, and how to set up a line of flight from a standard BASE jump exit, one that created a safe amount of separation from fixed objects and exit points, and one that enabled him to open his parachute in a hazard-free space.

When he sent me the video of his first wingsuit jump, I wasn't sure it was Johnny. He never showed his face. I recognized the way he held his fist when he fist-bumped the guy next to him that gave him instructions. Like any mother proud of her child's accomplishment, I congratulated him, told him he did a good job, and then told him to figure out how to show his face because that could be anyone jumping. He loved the experience, and I knew I'd be holding my breath quite often.

He stayed in Switzerland and traveled to Lauterbrunnen, a village nestled at the foot of towering rocky cliffs in the Alps. Johnny was sitting in the Horner Pub when he met one of his idols, an American big-wall rock climber, high-liner, and wingsuit BASE jumper, Dean Potter. Dean is a legend, not only for his action sports achievements, but for being a nonconformist and a rebel. His most infamous exploits involve wingsuit BASE jumping off of Yosemite Park's over-two-thousand-foot granite cliffs, which is illegal. Johnny approached Dean, offered to buy him a beer, and started a friendship.

He also met a gregarious Swiss wingsuit BASE jumper named Marco Regina. Marco invited him to Ticino, his home, to BASE jump there. They set their sights on jumping from Poncione D'Alnasca, a jagged 7,500-foot mountain.

On the day of the jump, they woke at four in the morning, spent seven hours hiking to the summit, jumped, and flew down the incredibly scenic river valley. When they landed in a soccer field, Johnny looked directly into his GoPro camera and called it, "The best day ever!"

Impressed by Johnny's flights, Gamma Labs signed on as his sponsor for a trip to Switzerland where Johnny produced the most impactful footage to date. When he returned home, he was asked to skydive for a Doritos commercial. Everything seemed to be going Johnny's way.

In January 2014, Johnny headed to Fiji, with his friend Jeb Corliss, on a trip sponsored by Gamma Labs. They wanted to capture extreme footage of wingsuit BASE jumping from a cliff on the island, but when they scouted the area via helicopter, they made the determination that it wasn't safe. Johnny said, "The best-case scenario would have been a painless death." But, in order to fulfill the agreement before he went back to classes at USC, Johnny and Jeb skydived from a helicopter wearing wingsuits. They soared high above the islands, creating beautiful, albeit less exciting, footage. I was happy that he was able to discern potentially fatal situations and pass on them. Perhaps this gave me a false sense of security in Johnny's wingsuit career; I always believed he'd make the right decisions to ensure his safety.

When Olivia was in her last year of high school, I started making plans for the empty-nest stage of my life. Ella was finishing law school, Johnny was at USC, and before long my youngest, Olivia, would be headed to a university. My empty-nest strategy included moving to the mountains somewhere and going for the Triple Crown—sometimes referred to as the Trilogy—of climbing. The Triple Crown entailed climbing Everest, Lhotse, and Nuptse—in a single season. I planned to do all three within three days. All three of those mountains form the horseshoe that is commonly seen in pictures of Everest. Everest is to the left, Lhotse in the middle, and Nuptse is to the right. At that point, no one had done all three in three days. I flipped my last house in Malibu and rented a home for the duration of Olivia's senior year.

I never thought I would be able to forgive my ex, and the thought of actually being friends with him was as distant as a far-off galaxy. It had been over ten years since our divorce, and we spoke only when it involved the children. Even at school functions, he barely made eye contact with me. But something changed in me while I was organizing bins of the kids' pictures in my garage. I found quite a few of him with his parents, his close friends from law school, and even some of him and a close friend who had passed away. Sitting alone on the floor, sorting through twenty-two years of the family pictures, I could have thrown them all away. A trashcan was within reach. No one would have ever known.

Then that voice in my head—the one I'd heard only heard twice before; the one that clearly saved my life—said, "Then you'd be the asshole." Deep in my soul I knew it wouldn't be right. I realized that the only one suffering from my anger was me.

I started putting baggies of photos into his mailbox. That simple gesture released something in me and made me feel like everything was okay. Years of lawsuits, insults, and fighting had taken their toll, and now this small token of neutrality planted a seed in my heart that allowed me to start healing.

Johnny had resumed classes at USC, and continued skydiving in his wingsuit every chance he got. In March, he was asked to speak at METAL International on a panel about defeating fear. Fear was something that he, and most extreme sports participants, don't concentrate on because they need their focus on achieving their goal and circumventing any potential issues. From the time he was a toddler sailing off the furniture, fear was an issue I rarely heard Johnny express, or even give a second thought to.

During his summer break from classes, Johnny headed to Norway for three weeks to wingsuit BASE jump and to participate in the World BASE Race, an annual event at Innfjorden where wingsuit BASE pilots compete against one another for top speed. The race starts with a qualification time trial in a timed solo jump. Johnny's time qualified him to move on to the next round:

a head-to-head competition with another wingsuit pilot where they jump from dual wooden platforms set side-by-side on the cliff top, and race to the ground. Johnny lost that round and was eliminated from the running for the championship. But, while in Norway, he took the most amazing proximity flying footage to date. He flew about one hundred miles per hour over a bridge full of spectators in Bispen. He had taken wingsuiting to the next level—proximity wingsuiting. His sponsor, Gamma Labs, was impressed with the video that Johnny had taken, showing him soaring perilously close to solid objects. I had mixed emotions as I watched his bird's eye view of jagged rock faces, towering conifers, and startled people on the bridge. His black and red wingsuit and parachute stood out against the stark natural features of Norway. I knew he loved what he was doing, and remembered the drawing he'd made of himself parachuting and eating ice cream. It was as if he was living up to his childhood vision.

I wasn't thrilled that he had taken up proximity flying and I didn't understand the ramifications of it, either. I don't think I fully comprehended the new, extreme version of wingsuiting, and maybe I didn't want to. I just knew that he flew closer to things. The idea of this sport is to utilize the wingsuit to fly extremely close to objects such as cliffs, trees, and anything else that is immovable. They do this in order to fully realize the speed at which they are flying. It takes the danger level of wingsuit BASE to a new dimension.

He left Norway and met up with Marco in Switzerland. While wingsuit BASE jumping, Marco had dislocated and broken his right shoulder, damaged the auxiliary nerve, and broken and compressed two vertebrae. The accident should have been fatal and, fortunately, it was an eye-opener for Marco, who told Johnny he'd quit the sport. The injury his friend had suffered didn't deter Johnny. When weather permitted, he jumped with his idol, Dean Potter, and sailed off the Via Ferrata, one of the more challenging jumps in Lauterbrunnen.

At the beginning of the fall semester, Johnny participated in the ALS Ice Bucket Challenge. That wasn't unusual, but he did it while skydiving, which made it very unique. He pursued every opportunity to jump and fly and decided to enter the World BASE Race again. He saw his greatest competition as Frode Johannessen, the three-time champion. In preparation, Johnny had his racing wingsuit modified to give him more speed. He also picked up his first official wingsuit equipment sponsor: Apex, which made the canopy—better known as a parachute—and the container that holds the canopy.

For my forty-ninth birthday, Johnny and I met in Palm Springs to climb the Cactus to Clouds trail on Mount San Jacinto. Johnny was fully into training for the Navy SEALs. I still was never sure when he was going to enlist, but he was training hard for the moment he did. We started around seven thirty in the morning; I was staying in Palm Springs so Olivia and her boyfriend could attend the Coachella Valley Music and Arts Festival, and Johnny drove in from his apartment at USC. During the climb, Johnny would stop and talk to almost everyone. He is far chattier than I. My back was killing me, and every hour or so, I would have to lie down on the trail to stretch my back out. We didn't bring enough water, as I was slowing us down and making the hike take longer than it should have.

While sharing our last water bottle, I brought up wingsuiting and how dangerous it was. I told him that if he died, my life would be over. He shot that captivating smile in my direction and explained that, if he died wingsuiting, that he would have died the happiest person on the planet. He said that it is the fastest death a person can have. There is no pain and, until the moment of death, you are having the most fun a person can have in the world. And basically, he wasn't going to quit. I prayed the Navy would make him quit—that somewhere in the fine print of whatever enlistment contract he signed, it forbade wingsuiting.

When we finally got to the top of San Jacinto, we grabbed some burgers for lunch and sat talking. Johnny was bummed that it had taken us so long, and I felt badly that I had slowed us down, even though on the way up, we were frequently passing people who had started hours before us. Johnny was slightly confused by this. Behind us were some guys talking loudly enough so that everyone could hear them bragging about how they had climbed up and not taken the aerial tram, and how fast they had done it. I looked at

Johnny and said, "I'm going to throw our trash away. While I'm gone, ask them how long they took to do the climb." When I got back, Johnny had a smile on his face. Johnny and his very slow mom had beaten their time by well over an hour.

Ella had graduated from law school, Olivia had graduated from high school, and Johnny was living on his own, still attending USC. I was now officially an empty-nester. I had only two requirements for my new home: it had to be within an easy drive of an international airport, and there had to be mountains. Tracy Murgatroyd invited me to Park City for the weekend to check out the area. It had been years since I was last there, and it was completely off my radar. She picked me up curbside at Salt Lake International Airport, a small airport that was easy to access. Ten minutes later, we were driving up the canyon to Park City. It was June and everything was green. Twenty-seven minutes from the airport, we were at her house in the heart of Park City. I was sold. Actually, I was sold by the time we hit Lamb's Canyon. After many years of drought, Malibu's hills were brown and dry. This was the complete opposite. "Things are either white or green," Tracy said, as I marveled at all the greenery.

I found a place and settled in. I spent my days hiking with my dogs, mountain biking in the hills that surround the town, and having small dinner parties on the deck with visiting friends and neighbors. I was seriously happy for the first time in a long time. I also went back to Kilimanjaro for my sixth time, climbing with a bunch of friends. I loved the quiet afternoons sitting on the porch with my two cats and two dogs watching the biggest rainstorms, echoing with thunder and illuminating the sky with lightning. It was an almost perfect summer. Life was good.

Johnny spent the summer training in California with one of America's top skydivers and wingsuit BASE jumpers, John Devore. John had more than twenty thousand jumps under his belt and had secured a prime sponsorship with Red Bull. While Johnny was there, he garnered a second sponsor, Tony Wingsuits of Zephyrhills, Florida, a wingsuit designer and manufacturer. Between training sessions, he spoke about his adventurous life at the Malibu

Library Speaker Series and trained to take the physical aptitude test to enter boot camp. He still held the goal of becoming a Navy SEAL after graduation.

And then, something shifted for him that summer. He experienced the back-to-back deaths of two of his wingsuit BASE jump heroes: Jhonathan Florez, also known as Jhonny Flowers, and his good friend and mentor, Dean Potter. Rather than being deterred by the deaths, Johnny decided not to enlist in the Navy. Instead, he decided that he wanted to be a full-time, professional wingsuit BASE jumper and proximity flyer.

While Johnny was pursuing his dream, the rest of the family was planning Ella's September wedding. She'd become engaged during her last year of law school and planned to marry after she took the New York Bar exam that summer. Unexpectedly, I had become friends with my ex's new wife at Ella's law school graduation. I'd invited her to Ella's bridal shower and invited her and my ex to a U2 concert. I had an opportunity to get to know her children and thought they were wonderful.

Life seemed to be going so well. Ella had passed the bar exam, Olivia had settled on Georgetown University, and Johnny was happily wingsuiting. I was living in a charming mountain ski town and was dating someone I thought might be "the one."

I probably should have paid more attention to, or been more cognizant of, the little things that popped up in my life. One of them happened while I was breaking down moving boxes in my garage. A lone dove flew into the garage and simply sat on the windowsill for about an hour. I finished with the boxes and had to leave the garage door open so he could fly out. I have always seen these birds in pairs and never alone. I wasn't sure what it meant, but it stuck out in my mind and didn't sit right with me.

I had a dream that was disturbing. It was about a nanny the children had on a vacation, and she was chasing Johnny and me on a skateboard. In the dream, she represented death. I was unnerved and reminded myself it was only a dream. It didn't make any sense because Johnny was no longer a child, he didn't need a nanny, and he was doing very well.

Another thing happened when Brian and Chris MacGregor came to visit. We were driving, and Chris asked me point-blank about Johnny's extreme sport and whether I understood the risk. I told her I understood the dangers and emphasized that he would be fine. He was good at what he did and, hopefully, he'd quit as soon as he got married or something else distracted him from BASE jumping. All three of those little incidents left me feeling that I needed to be more aware, more alert to something—but I didn't know what it was. I refused to let it wear on me, with all the great things happening in our lives.

Chapter 10

Johnny and I walking down the aisle
at Ella's wedding, Santa Ynez, CA.

Ella's wedding was beautiful, as we all expected. Dashing in a gray suit, my beautiful son escorted me down the aisle to my seat. He was no longer my little muffin man, the one who couldn't fall asleep at night unless our heads were touching. My little boy had grown up to be an amazing twenty-three-year-old man. I was proud of all of my children, and that day cemented that feeling in my heart.

Johnny had planned another trip to Europe after the wedding. It was sponsored by Gamma Labs, which wanted to produce a documentary with Johnny's footage. The modern sport of wingsuiting became mainstream in the late 1990s and early 2000s primarily because skydivers were in search of longer-lasting flights. A wingsuit allows those who are free-falling to glide or "fly" farther and for an extended period of time. After one of his trips, Johnny had told me that for every foot you drop, you are able to glide three feet wearing a wingsuit. He had really studied the sport and, in a way, I could understand his desire to create a more exhilarating experience.

I knew wingsuiting wasn't a sport that you woke up one day and decided to try. I knew it took tremendous physical and mental strength and skills to succeed, and that it required a long progression of learning and training. For Johnny it started with skydiving, something he'd begged his father and me to let him do since he was a young boy. He'd been paragliding since he was fourteen and skydiving since he turned eighteen. That was fun to a point, but there was always a desire to reach the next level. For Johnny, that next level was BASE jumping, which a jumper can only attempt after a certain number of jumps from an airplane. From there it is wearing a wingsuit out of an airplane for a certain number of jumps, learning how to fly while wearing the suit, and then jumping out of a hot-air balloon if you happen to have access to one. It all takes years before someone wingsuits from the edge of a cliff. And even that thrill/rush/skill isn't enough for some.

My phone rang as I was walking into a yoga class. I missed the call but saw Johnny had left a message. I walked outside to call him back.

"Hi Mommy, I'm leaving for Europe," he said.

I loved it when he called me "Mommy," and the fact that he had no problem telling me he loved me, no matter who was around or where we were. I asked him if he needed anything—was he okay with money, did he have everything for the trip? He told me that he had everything he needed and that his sponsors were paying for everything. He said he would be coming to Utah to visit me when he got back. He wanted to see me, of course, but also because I lived in one of the only states that legally allowed BASE jumping. I told him I loved him and to be safe.

We hung up and I cried, which didn't make sense to me. I never cried, no matter how far away my children ventured. I was always happy for them when they traveled. I knew they were having wonderful experiences that would add to their life lessons. I had a rule to never call Johnny when he was away on this wingsuiting trips because I was always concerned about calling at the wrong moment. I worried that his cell would ring while he was on the edge of a cliff, distract him, and he'd lose his concentration.

Johnny had posted an image of himself wingsuiting in Switzerland, flying a foot above the trees, and captioned it, "Carving down the mountain today in my Jedei 2 #wingsuit #HyperDrive."

The photo was jarring. I had never seen him fly this close to the ground. I was used to seeing photos and videos of him leaping out of airplanes, helicopters, and hot-air balloons, and off bridges. Proximity wingsuiting is seeing just how close you can get to other objects, while flying close to that object at over a hundred mph. This is what gave BASE jumpers an even bigger thrill and an even faster sense of speed. The closer you are to the object, the more you feel the speed. And the less chance there is to correct any error.

The image he posted was truly proximity wingsuit BASE jumping. It was undeniably the next level, and I couldn't help but fixate on the picture. He was flying so close to the treetops that it looked as though he could reach out and touch them. Johnny was perfectly horizontal, flying, arms spread wide like a bird. The sky was clear and blue. His black and red wingsuit contrasted against the gray of the sharp granite cliffs behind him. His black, full-face helmet held his GoPro in front of it.

His friends had commented on the image with statements such as, "Perfect," "Awesome," and his sister, Ella, wrote, "Be careful!!! Love you." The comments didn't mean much to me; I was too captivated by the photo.

Greg, my boyfriend at the time, told me to stop staring at the picture. "He isn't going to die doing that," he said. "Dying that way is not his path."

He's right, I thought. I put my phone away, feeling embarrassed and rude for staring at it during dinner. Still, it was difficult to turn away from my phone and the image on it. I relied on the fact that I knew my son was an amazingly competent wingsuit pilot, a serious athlete, confident about his abilities, and knowledgeable about the science behind it.

I normally woke up and the first thing I did was look at my cell phone. I didn't that morning as I'd dropped it into a toilet the day before and left it sitting in a bag of rice overnight to dry out. I took it out of the bag, not knowing if it would work or not, and headed out the door of Greg's house. I felt happy, content and settled. I was forty-nine and maybe that's what forty-nine-year-olds did? They settled. I got into my car, plugged my phone into the USB, and started the thirty-five-minute drive from Salt Lake City to my home in Park City. Going sixty miles an hour with the flow of traffic in the fast lane on the 15 South, I jumped when my phone rang.

I recognized the number immediately. It was my ex-husband's landline in Malibu. My brain went into hyperdrive. Why would he be calling me? I knew it couldn't be Ella calling, as she was just arriving home in Brooklyn, New York from her mini honeymoon. It couldn't be my youngest, Olivia, as she was also on the East Coast and not in Malibu. Why would my ex be calling me at seven thirty in the morning Pacific Time? I hesitated. I knew instinctively that I didn't want to know.

"Why are you calling me?" was how I answered the phone.

"Johnny," is all he could say.

"Oh my God, I forgot to renew his Global Rescue insurance. This is going to cost a lot of money to get him home on a medical flight." I rambled, willing that scenario into reality.

"No," he started.

I don't remember the rest of what he said. I literally felt like some imaginary walls had closed in around me. My gorgeous, funny, smart, handsome, bright, confident, strong, baby boy, my little muffin man, was dead at twenty-three.

He died while wingsuiting off a mountain in Switzerland. I started screaming, and somehow managed to cross three lanes of traffic to pull over to the side of the freeway. A police officer in an unmarked car pulled over after I flashed my lights at him. I'm not sure how I even knew it was a police officer. I couldn't breathe; I was screaming. The officer asked if I had just received bad news. I cried, "My son just died." My ex was still on the phone with me when the officer tried to take the keys out of the ignition. He asked me to get into his car and said he was afraid that I would run into the traffic.

I cried, "I'm not suicidal. Don't disconnect my phone call." Ella's number showed on the screen of my phone. I put my ex on hold even though I knew I couldn't tell her what had happened. I was crying and could only utter the words, "Call your dad."

She said, "What? What?"

I couldn't tell her. I hung up. The officer walked me back to his car and I got into the front passenger seat. I tried showing him pictures of Johnny, but the water-damaged phone wouldn't let me pull any up. I asked him if he had kids. He nodded, and I defiantly told him he should teach them how to golf. Weird, random things come out of your mouth when you're in shock. Greg pulled up behind the unmarked car parked behind mine on the side of the freeway. Someone had called him to come and get me.

The officer suggested that we leave my car there because I was in no condition to drive. Greg stupidly and selfishly responded, "She can drive."

The officer looked at him with a quizzical look while I, oblivious to the officer's concern for me, got in my car. The officer followed us to Greg's office, and we drove to my house from there in his car. When we arrived at my home, I was numb and thankful to learn that my ex-husband had arranged a flight that would get me to LA later that afternoon.

I managed to reach Alex, the young man who was with Johnny on that last jump. He answered his phone while in the police station in Canton Uri. His voice was shaky as he replied to my questions. It had been just the two of them for that jump. Alex had leapt from the cliff two seconds after Johnny and both of them had filmed the entire thing.

I asked him where Johnny was. He said, "On the mountain. Search and Rescue has a helicopter, but it can't fly due to weather."

I had seen dead bodies on Everest. The thought of my son, alone and cold on a mountain, was more than I could bear. I started screaming at him not to leave my son alone up there on the mountain. I told him to go back up there to be with him. He lied and said he would. Before the police confiscated Alex's phone and GoPro, he told me there would be a full investigation, and that he had been able to download the final pictures taken before the jump.

Everything felt surreal. I needed to take a shower, but water makes you feel something and I didn't want to feel anything. The water opened an emotional flood of tears, just as I thought it would. I got out of the shower and lay on my bed with the dogs. They didn't understand why I was crying. They remained still and stayed by my side until we needed to leave for the airport. I wondered, how was I in this situation?

I was in this situation because my son chose to proximity wingsuit BASE jump.

The woman at the airline counter allowed Greg to accompany me to the gate. I had checked a bag of clothes and kept with me the carry-on that was filled to capacity with pictures of Johnny. In the waiting area, a man walked over and handed me some tissues.

Greg harshly declared, "She's upset because her son just died," as casually as if he were telling someone what he ate for dinner last night. The man looked apologetically at me. I couldn't tell if it was because he was sorry my son had just died, or if he felt badly for me that I was with such a buffoon.

My ex had put me in first class, which was incredibly kind of him. I sat next to the window, trying to hold myself together, and immediately felt sorry for the man who sat down next to me. I knew that if I cried hysterically on the plane, they wouldn't let me fly. I kept it together long enough for the plane to take off; then I couldn't stop sobbing. The man seated next to me politely tried to ignore me. I was sure he thought I was crazy.

The things you think about when your whole life has just fallen apart are odd. When I got into the police car on the freeway, I wondered if people thought I was being arrested. Now I was wondering if the man next to me thought I was crazy. I had long ago given up caring what people thought of me. Why was it so important now?

I apologized and told him I wasn't crazy. I showed him a picture of my son on my new iPhone, and then I told him my son had died. He handed me his ear buds and his iPad and played Andrea Bocelli's "The Prayer." I hit the repeat button for an hour and a half as tears streamed down my face. The song was so comforting.

This saint of a man escorted me off the plane, held my purse, and watched my suitcase full of pictures, my most valued possession in the world at this point, while I used the ladies' room. He walked me to the curb and waited with me until my friends arrived. When they did, he walked away, turned back toward me, and waved. I didn't even know his name, and yet I will forever be grateful to this complete stranger's act of kindness.

I climbed into Jerri Churchill's truck. Inez McGee and Kelly Chapman Meyer had come with her. Jerri got lost leaving the airport and we turned the truck around. We saw my ex, his wife, and Ella, who had already arrived. Olivia would be landing shortly, and they were waiting on the side of Sepulveda Boulevard. We pulled up behind his car.

My friends got out of the truck and stood on the sidewalk while my ex stepped into the back seat. His face was tear-stained. I climbed on top of him, literally straddling him, as I grabbed his face with both of my hands, screaming at him that it wasn't his fault, and that Johnny was lucky to have him as a father. He couldn't stop crying and blaming himself for Johnny's death. I knew there was zero chance on this earth that he was at fault for this. Johnny had always known what he was going to do and no one could ever stop him. I couldn't dissuade him. I'd tried. No amount of my ex's money could bribe him to stop jumping off cliffs. We had nothing that Johnny wanted. Logic never prevailed. There was no way that either of us could control Johnny. He was his own man.

One of those small crazy thoughts that go through your mind left me wondering if his wife would be mad at me for straddling her husband in the back of a truck and yelling at him. I wanted to convince him that none of this was his doing. Unfortunately, he couldn't hear a word of it. Neither of us was coherently processing our thoughts.

I prayed for the day that everyone understood that it was no one's fault, including my own, for not teaching my son golf, or tennis, or something else tame. I also prayed that my ex knew that I would do anything for him. He's the father of my incredible children and he was a good parent.

Olivia's flight landed, and she joined us on the side of the road. One of the girls rode with my friends and me to my ex's house in Malibu. I don't remember which one. I don't recall the drive to Malibu. I think I was lying down in the back seat. I do remember walking into my ex's house, which was filled with people.

I was thankful when I learned that my daughters had each experienced similar acts of kindness on their flights to California. Olivia was given anti-nausea medication by someone on board her flight, and Ella had been taken care of by people in the airport who helped her get to her plane. The caring kindnesses of people you don't even know can alleviate the weight of a horrible trauma and make it seem a little easier to deal with. I prayed that if I was ever seated next to someone who needed help, I would behave the same way my angel and my daughters' angels had. Their actions were truly a gift of comfort and solace that we desperately needed at that time.

I was staying at my ex's home, and at one point, while sitting in the backyard, a young man came up behind me and put his face next to mine and tried to hug me. I realized it was Trevor Jacob, Johnny's best friend since grade school. I couldn't help myself; I stood up and shoved him so hard he should have fallen over.

"You're next!" I yelled at him. I screamed, "Do you see this?" as I made a sweeping gesture with my arms to everyone standing around. "Is this what you want for your parents?" I was crying and then hugged him hard and tight, as I sobbed.

Lynn and Jerry, his parents, were standing behind me, watching the whole thing. The next day I apologized to them for assaulting their son. Lynn told me she was happy that I'd said what I had, as she couldn't convince him to stop participating in extreme sports. He was an Olympic competitor in snowboarding, so he, too, was a highly trained professional athlete. Trevor parachuted, took part in many other highly dangerous sports, and BASE jumped. But BASE jumping doesn't care who you are or how skilled you are. I was relieved when I heard that he'd sold his wingsuit and stopped BASE jumping, even though he continued to skydive.

Chapter 11

Paddle-out for Johnny. Zuma Beach, California

The next twelve days were a blur. Thoughts of killing myself were never far away, as I just wanted to be with Johnny. I was engulfed in grief. Thankfully, those suicidal moments didn't last long. I had two beautiful daughters there in front of me, and a son who wasn't. I could have had fifteen children. It wouldn't have mattered. When you lose a child, your soul is crushed. It's unacceptable on every level, and the desire to be with the one who is gone, if only for a brief moment, overpowers life. I longed for one last hug, to hear the sound of his voice, his laugh, and to hear him call me Mommy.

Every morning, I woke up to the nightmare that wouldn't go away. Endless cups of coffee, followed by whatever drugs my friends handed me, followed by endless glasses of wine, had no effect. No matter what I drank or took, I couldn't escape this horrific scene that was now my life.

The people around me, friends, some close, some acquaintances, and some I had just met, saved me, quite literally. I don't remember when the next-door neighbor, Chris Cortazzo, showed up that first night, but when I woke up that first morning, he had somehow wedged his buff, six-foot, two-inch frame in between my oldest daughter and me on Johnny's full-size mattress to keep us safe and comforted all night. He and Ella were the reasons I didn't kill myself that first morning. I didn't want them to see all of the blood and mess if I slit my wrists with something from Johnny's sword collection that hung above the bed. I went outside to scream instead.

The women who surrounded me at the dining room table every day talked among themselves because I was barely coherent. The collective energy from them literally kept me from falling deeper into that crevasse of grief. I could physically feel their energy supporting me, allowing me to mourn in any way I needed. They brought in food and created schedules to keep me company so I wouldn't be alone. Emotionally they were there for all of us, without judgment. Their support and the fact that they were there helped all of us.

For me, time seemed to stand still, and yet I was furious that time went on without my son. I felt like my life had stopped, and I expected the world to stop, too. I was frustrated and angry at life and the hand it had dealt, but I couldn't be mad at Johnny. I could never be mad at him. By age twenty-three, Johnny had lived the life of an octogenarian. He was the most pure and authentic soul I ever knew. I'd always said, "It's good to be Johnny Strange." And it was. He was our adored only son who was sandwiched in between two very intelligent, beautiful sisters. His sense of freedom and independence was not an easy thing with a dad who prized school above all else. Johnny found his intelligence in all things sports—namely, extreme sports. I couldn't be angry at a sport my son loved so much. I certainly couldn't be mad at the wind, which is what killed him. I could, however, be mad at the man I was dating.

A day or two after Johnny died, Greg flew in to be with me. His behavior during the ten days he was in Malibu to "support" me was sick beyond measure. He gave us all someone/something to be angry with.

We spent one night together at my former husband's home, and Greg complained about having to sleep in my dead son's bed at my ex-husband's house. We moved our things over to Chris Cortazzo's house next door. The first morning I woke up there, I was overcome with joy. I had had a dream about Johnny and excitedly shared it with him. In my dream Johnny progressed from a baby whose belly I was blowing raspberries on to him as a middle-schooler.

Greg's response was, "I had a dream I was licking you. Is that ever going to happen again?" Followed later by, "You smell. You need to take a shower."

What was I doing with a man like this? How had I not seen who he really was? A few days later, he was angry because he wanted to have a "date" night. I could barely get out of bed, and he was annoyed because he wanted to go out on the town in Malibu and I wasn't up for it. He made a comment to some friends that I was no longer the woman he'd first met, and if I didn't snap out of it, he didn't see a future for us. They were shocked by his callousness and self-centered behavior, especially at a time like this. His bad behavior didn't stop there. I couldn't get him to stop taking interior pictures of my friend's homes and posting some personal pictures on social media. The man had no respect for personal boundaries.

To get us out of the house for a while, Chris Cortazzo suggested we go to the beach and enjoy the water and the sun. Emotionally, I was running on empty, and just followed the directions of others. Chris and I swam out into the big waves, which no longer seemed scary to me. I used to dread being in the ocean, but now I felt nothing.

Normally I am terrified of sharks and dark water. Now, I had zero cares or worries about any of that. To me, drowning would have been a relief at that moment, and I actually prayed for a shark to swallow me whole.

Greg swam out to join us. To me, it seemed like an egotistical effort to show off to the locals when he swam out toward the bigger waves. Chris and I swam back to the shore, sat on the sand, and watched him get pummeled by wave after wave. Chris, a former lifeguard, was concerned for his safety. I had no empathy for what he was putting himself through. I couldn't even relate to him as a fellow human.

The entire family decided to get tattoos to honor and celebrate Johnny. We felt it was a fitting tribute and a reminder that he would always be with each of us. While we paid homage to Johnny, Greg made certain everyone knew how bored he was. At lunch afterwards, he finished his drink and then posted a picture of an empty glass with a tag that read something like, "I'm done." I knew he wasn't referring to his drink. On the drive back to Malibu, we all squeezed tightly into the Suburban. I sat on the floor between the second-row seats when that callous individual I had once cared about made the announcement, "Eighty people died in Syria today. No one seems to care about them. You know, one person's life isn't more important than someone else's."

I was appalled, speechless and frozen by the insensitive cruelty he expressed at that particular time. To the credit of everyone, especially my ex, no one threw him out of the moving vehicle.

I kept my anger under wraps, as I knew I would break up with him the minute we returned to Utah. I didn't send him back to Park City as I should have because I had left some expensive and uninsured diamond earrings along with my car at his house. I was sure I would never see them again if I ended the relationship while he was in Malibu and sent him packing. Had I been thinking clearly, I would have sent someone to his house to retrieve my property. But I wasn't there yet. I didn't have the energy or mental presence to send him packing, or to ask someone to pick up my things. Fortunately, my friends' husbands ran interference for me and tried to keep him away from me as much as possible.

Johnny's death was all over the media. Fox News, CNN, CBS Los Angeles, *The Today Show*, and a segment on NBC called "Dying to Fly" all incorporated it into their news. The *Malibu Times* ran "Malibu-based athlete Johnny Strange Dies" and the *LA Times* version read, "BASE-Jumper Johnny Strange dies in wingsuit jump in Swiss Alps." His name and photographs were everywhere online, including places none of us would ever have expected to look, like *Maxim*, *Outside*, *E! News*, and *US Weekly*'s celebrity news: "Johnny Strange, Famed Adventurer, Dies at 23 in Wingsuiting Accident." Olivia and Ella kept me apprised of the coverage. I couldn't watch it or read it because they were talking about my child, and I refused to accept that their stories and reports were true. The finality of the accident that resulted in his death was, to me, not based in reality.

Within two days of Johnny's passing, Trevor Jacob had organized a paddle-out for Johnny at Zuma Beach. A paddle-out is a way of honoring someone after they have died. It's a large circle of people, mainly on surfboards, who form a group just past the surf break. I really felt a need to be with anyone who loved Johnny because I was still a living, walking zombie. I looked forward to getting into the ocean and connecting with his friends. Kelly Chapman Meyer picked me up and brought five standup paddleboards, which she'd loaded into the back of her big black truck. As we drove to the beach, I lay down in the back seat. Sitting up was too exhausting. We pulled into the Zuma Beach parking lot, and I sat up and asked if there was a triathlon or marathon going on. The parking lot was full and hundreds of people had gathered, which was unusual for Zuma Beach at that time of day in October.

Kelly replied, "No. This is for Johnny's paddle-out."

I was stunned. I got out of the truck, wearing a blue and white one-piece that I had borrowed from Olivia. I hadn't been able to open the suitcase that I'd brought to Malibu from Park City. The suitcase and everything in it reminded me of that horrible morning only three days earlier. The water was quite cold, but I didn't bother wearing a wetsuit. I wanted to feel the cold, I wanted to freeze. I wanted to feel something, anything.

The waves were big. I stood on my board and started to paddle out, but I didn't have the energy or strength to navigate the force of the waves. I dove off the board and the person escorting me out took my board and paddle and moved them past the break for me. I swam under a few waves and once past the break, got back onto the board.

There were so many kind and helpful people in the water that day. Lydia Rink Stiegler was in the water, holding my board in place, once I was in the circle. Behind me was a lifeguard boat. Fitting, I thought, since I still considered drowning myself a good option. Then, out of nowhere, an arm with the words "Cynthia Rowley" emblazoned on the wetsuit appeared. I immediately thought, *Hmmm, I didn't know she made wetsuits.* The arm belonged to Kelly. I smiled. The thought of Kelly wearing a designer wetsuit made me laugh inside. I knew then that I would make it through this nightmare, even if I didn't really want to.

I sat on the board in the cold water, shivering, watching all of these amazing people show up for Johnny. My daughters, my ex and his wife, and Johnny's girlfriend, Piper, were next to me. Trevor spoke, as did Ted Silverberg. I have no recollection of what was said. I didn't want to be there, acknowledging that he was gone. Being there was admitting that Johnny was dead. I wasn't ready to face that yet.

Once the speeches were over and people started paddling back in, I saw how many people were actually there. People who had known Johnny and our family for over two decades showed up. Thomas Muselli rode his horse along the beach, carrying the American flag. So many people were in the water, and about the same number were standing on the beach throwing flowers into the water. A local news crew was there. Johnny made the six o'clock news again. I told the newsperson that I just wanted my son home. That statement was very real to me, although I knew it might sound delusional to the reporter. Johnny was technically still in Switzerland. I wanted his body, his ashes, to be home in Malibu. I didn't want him to be so far away. Practically catatonic, I don't remember leaving the paddle-out and going back to the house.

Days wore on. The Swiss recovered Johnny's body but not his GoPro camera, which probably filmed everything. I suppose it was a small blessing in disguise. I don't know that I would have survived watching his footage. Seeing most of his last flight on Alex's GoPro was difficult enough. I couldn't watch past the three-second mark. I never will. My ex and his wife flew to Switzerland to pick up our son while I stayed behind with the girls. Olivia hadn't brought her passport, which meant to my irrational mind that we couldn't all go together to get him. Had I been thinking analytically, I would have flown with Olivia to pick her passport up and met the rest of the family in Switzerland. There was another fear that crept in, too. I was terrified that if I went and left the girls in Malibu, the plane might crash and my beautiful daughters would be orphaned. There is a part of me that will forever regret not going to get my child; not being able to hold him one last time…

I silently sat at the dining room table surrounded by my friends when they returned from Switzerland with Johnny's belongings and his ashes. The Swiss had released everything except for his wingsuit, parachute, and helmet. They promised to ship it to us once the Swiss police had completed their investigation. My friends got up to leave and give us privacy. My ex called the girls, Ella's then-husband, Piper, and me into the family room. I grabbed my friend Chris MacGregor. I didn't want her to leave; I wanted someone there with me. She and I had the same awful thought going through our heads: We had always believed we would be doing this for her child first, her daughter with cystic fibrosis. Even though she had brought Johnny's dangerous sport and its consequences up to me two days before he died, we never thought Johnny would die first.

The urn was placed on the coffee table. I knew what was inside it—I just couldn't fathom it. I couldn't look at it. I was present but not there. My body felt heavy and my legs felt weak. I could barely breathe.

My ex and his wife sank into one end of the L-shaped couch, exhausted from the trip and the emotional depletion of Johnny's death. I sat down on the other side next to Piper, while Chris stood behind me. I knew she didn't want to be in that room, none of us did, but Chris is undoubtedly one of the strongest women I know, so she stayed, knowing that I needed the support of my good friend.

I turned to Piper, Johnny's girlfriend, and said, "Don't take this the wrong way, but if Johnny had ended up a fifty-year-old-man with two kids working nine to five, he'd have been miserable." Tears streamed down her face, but she managed a small smile in acknowledgement.

Then she was asked, "You wouldn't happen to be pregnant, would you?" I felt a tiny light of hope in my heart. Piper shook her head and my heart sank once again.

Johnny's duffel bag lay on the floor. The girls sat next to it. Olivia unzipped it and pulled out Johnny's laptop. His phone was there, too. It was smashed into a million pieces. His phone was the only thing the authorities had not kept. Johnny's German Shepherds wouldn't get off of his well-worn duffle bag. They were as sad and confused as the rest of us. Olivia opened Johnny's laptop and the first thing that came up was an essay he had written right before he left for this final trip. These are his exact words:

"Why I BASE jump:

"As I get ready to leave again on another wingsuit BASE jumping trip, it's probably important to write down why I like to do this. With all the death in the sport, people always ask me why I don't quit or think I'm crazy. Imagine though, if you could pick up your phone and text any hero or role model you ever had, and not only be able to text them, but be friends with them too.

"I walked into Apex base (gear sponsor) and they gave me a Lobo parachute to use on my trip. Imagine walking into a Ferrari dealership, being on a first name basis with the owner and having him hand you the keys to one for free. There is no greater feeling than proximity flying wing suits. The only thing similar is big wave surfing, and if you're thinking it has something to do with fear and adrenaline you are completely wrong. It's a total misconception, at least how I view it. Flying down a mountain makes you present in a way that can't be described, completely in tune with nature. A monk meditates his whole life to reach a point I feel I've captured while racing though mountains powered purely by gravity and intuition. When I hear people say, "If I die doing it, it's worth it" I cringe. If I were to die flying, it would not be worth it. Life is the most precious thing on the planet, and flying brings out the absolute best in life. If you die proximity flying however, you die twice. Once physically, the other is the death of your legacy. The public outside of our community may love watching the videos, but if the worst happens the comment section on the articles show no respect. I remember after Dean died, someone who had lived more of a life than most could imagine, was viciously attacked on how he lived. If you eat until you're fat and die of a heart attack it's a tragedy, but if you die on the cutting edge of imagination, you're an idiot. I watched people attack Dean after his death without him able to defend himself, and I'm sure the same would happen to me. They would say I should have died on Everest; they would say flying wing suits was insanity. But with everything going on in the world, I can say I have things that make me happy, experiences that you can't buy."

Reading his words about something he truly loved doing was both painful and powerful. Did he somehow know or have a feeling that he wouldn't survive?

Was it his intuition speaking? Was he trying to tell us that it was all right when each of us knew it wasn't?

I didn't want to be there. My mind filled with questions. I felt as though I was experiencing some strange parallel universe. Where was Johnny? When was he coming home? Every minute of every hour had been excruciatingly painful since I first received news of his death. How would I go on living like this? How would I go on without him, his voice, his presence, his magnetic smile, and his energy? I was scared that this type of pain would never go away. I wondered if Johnny could ever have stopped flying. Could I ever stop climbing and racing? Then, through my cluttered mind, a simple question to myself came through clearly. If I kept climbing, would I hear or see Johnny while climbing or racing?

I had brought the contents of the "Johnny" photo bin with me from Park City, and I busied myself sorting the images. For me, it was much easier to exist in the past than in the current moment. I set aside a of pile of photographs of my former husband and Johnny, so that he would have those treasures.

A photo of Johnny as a twelve-year-old hung in the living room. In it, he stood next to his father with a serious look on his face. He looked so little in that picture. The photo was part of an article that had been written about them as a father-son mountain climbing duo. The story reported that Johnny had summited Mount Vinson, the highest mountain in Antarctica, with his dad, setting a world record as the youngest person ever to do so. I smiled, knowing that he will have that record forever, as there is now a rule that no one under sixteen is allowed to attempt that climb.

The yellow ice axe in the photo went with Johnny on every one of his climbs, even on the ones that didn't require ice axes. I had suggested burying it near the crash site, but his father said that we should save it for our grandkids. He was right. I looked at the picture and wondered if someday one of my grandkids would climb with it on some grand mountain.

I lost myself in memories exposed by the photographs while the girls scoured Johnny's computer. They found a second essay. I felt as if he wrote these essays to and for each of us, so that we understood him better. It was as if he needed to explain the things we refused to see and acknowledge. This essay made it clear to me that he didn't take flying lightly. He had worried about and considered the impact on others in his choices and understood why we couldn't comprehend the magnetic pull flying had on him. Yet, none of what he expressed was enough to make him stop flying. He wrote:

Once you jump you are never the same. All it takes is one second for your entire life to change, for everything to seem incomparable to those ten to fifteen seconds flying through the air. Once you jump, no one you care about is ever the same. It's not that I don't know this and understand it, it's that I physically can't stop. If I were to stop, my life would be meaningless. I know this because I've tried. I tried school, I tried school for six years at the University of Southern California. I studied international relations, I went to class, I joined a fraternity, I tried to be what I knew my family wanted, a normal son in college. I just wanted to make my dad and my older sister proud. They are seriously the two smartest people that I know.

As I sit on the couch with this beautiful girl snuggled up next to me on one side and my little sister on the side and I get frustrated with them for not understanding the historical context of "The Devil's Double" the thought flashes before me. Out of everything, this is what I'm scared of. I love these people, this life, these stupid arguments and spending all of my weekend watching movies with Piper in the dark room with Ashton and Olivia coming in and out. I'm not scared of flying, I'm not scared of dying, I'm scared of loving these people. I'm scared of the day they lose me. I'm scared because I know they'll hurt, I know they'll miss me, and I know they'll think that I didn't care enough about them to stop jumping, That's the worst part. I wish I could make them understand without having them jump. If I had a son of my own, I would pray inside that he never jumped, but once he did, I would know that there is nothing I can possibly do to stop him.

I felt as though he was reaffirming to each one of us that his death wasn't anyone's fault. It was Johnny just being his honest self, examining all the possibilities, taking no shortcuts, and sending us a strong message from his heart that he loved us as much as we loved him.

We had wanted to blame his accident on equipment failure, but we were told that the cause was merely a gust of wind. Johnny had been hit by a gust and because he was so close to the cliff, there was no time to make any corrections. He crashed into a cliff on Mount Gitschen eight seconds after he left the cliff's edge. He had never had the chance to deploy his chute. It was an accident and the cause was nature.

The morning of Johnny's memorial, I could barely drag myself from the bed. I was playing mental games with myself and thought that, if I didn't attend the memorial service, then none of this would have really happened. Even the glass of wine I had when I showed up to the restaurant that hosted it didn't make a dent in my anger and grief. All I wanted was for the man I was seeing to leave me alone and for me to not be living a life that no longer had Johnny in it.

Chapter 12

O n the following day, the morning of October 13, I flew back to Park City and immediately dumped what I had called a boyfriend. If my friends had not seen for themselves his incredibly poor behavior, they wouldn't have believed it. The way he acted the whole time he was in Malibu left me unable to imagine any sort of future with him, not even another day. He was out of my life.

I had recently bought a house that needed an extensive remodel. I threw myself into that, staying as physically busy as possible, until it felt like an acceptable hour to have a glass of wine or three. The hour that became acceptable was getting earlier and earlier. Thankfully, I had dogs to walk and bird feeders to fill. During one particularly low point, I was again contemplating suicide, and looked up from my fetal position on the living room floor to see all four of my animals staring at me. The energy, or lack of, that I was giving had to confuse my two cats and my dogs, Oliver and Lola. In my mind, I knew who would take each one of them and which ones my friends would fight over if I decided to leave this earth. Everyone would have a home except Oliver. He was a bit of a problem child. He'd been abused as a puppy, which left him food-obsessed, like no other animal I'd ever had. I was sure no one would take him, and the thought of my precious friend ending up in a shelter was unacceptable. So, instead of suicide, I went to bed. I told myself that I could rethink the suicide option in the morning.

Suicide continued to haunt my thoughts when I was too overwhelmed with life and the grief of losing Johnny. Trevor Jacob shared with me his thoughts on suicide: "F*** that place." That place was defined as that hole of grief or anxiety or despair for the future. I began to say those three words and focus on something else. I had to change my headspace. I realized that every day I made it through was a day to celebrate. I couldn't give in and quit. To me that was the most selfish thing a person could do to others, and yet, it sometimes seemed like the only way out. I knew then, as I know now, that it isn't. I also believed strongly that I would have to repeat all of this pain if I chose that way out. I believed that I would have to handle all of this trauma better in the next life, because I believe that we are here to learn lessons and grow as souls.

Slowly, like walking through molasses, I was able to continue on, getting through one day, and then another. On one particularly cold morning, while walking the dogs, I had an epiphany. It suddenly struck me that I wanted to live, not just exist. I went home from that walk and signed up for a hundred-and-fifty-five-mile ultra-run that was hosted by my friend Mary Gadam's company, Racing The Planet. The race was two months away, and it was to be held in Sri Lanka. I immediately limited my wine intake to one glass a day. I focused on getting in shape for this race, praying I might be able to see, feel, or hear Johnny somewhere in the jungle.

It felt good to be physically active again with a purpose. One night during the race, I looked up and saw a shooting star. I smiled and thought, there's my boy. I felt a connection with Johnny that sent waves of joy through my being. He had sent me a sign.

As I crossed the finish line, Mary hugged me and whispered in my ear, "You're back." I appreciated her words so much. I knew I wasn't back, but I had taken another small step up the mountain from the valley of grief. I was so grateful to her and her staff, and I was especially grateful to the Sri Lankan military man, John, who, on day two of the race, started running alongside me. I'm sure I slowed his pace considerably, yet he never left my side.

When I returned home, I fell back into the doldrums of grief. I wondered if things would ever be normal again. Every day seemed to drag on and on. Minutes often felt like hours. And the only thing I was excited about was when it was time to go to bed because there was always the possibility that I would have a dream about Johnny. Physical movement seemed to be my only salvation, unless the wave of grief hit, and then it would be nearly impossible to leave the house. Sometimes the only time I would go outside was to fill the bird feeders; that was nonnegotiable for me. I also had to shovel snow.

I avoided looking into any mirrors for months after he died; I couldn't face this new person who had lost her son. I felt haggard and old. I tried to remind myself of fun things to come in the future, the possibilities that life still had to offer. One morning I had a conversation with myself. "Maybe I should

take antidepressants," I told myself. "Maybe you should get your fat ass off
this couch and go on a hike," I replied. I would have been wise to listen to the
latter. I was barely going through the motions of life and realized that staying
home alone gave me too much unoccupied time to think. I escaped by getting
on airplanes to visit my girls or friends. Before one flight, I downed a Bloody
Mary and a chardonnay, and I found myself not caring about anything.

Whenever I spoke with my daughters, I was always relieved to know they were
muddling through better than I. They are both so strong and independent, but
I knew the loss of their brother was almost unbearable for them.

Olivia had returned to Georgetown and was allowed, as a freshman, her
own dorm room. She needed and wanted to be alone, and I understood that
desire because I had it, too. One minute, I could be laughing and the very
next, I'd be a sobbing mess. It was so hard to be around other people, keep up
appearances, and manage any semblance of social skills. Add the pressure of
college onto to the emotional fatigue, and I was impressed with her ability to
balance it all. Then Georgetown University allowed her to have a cat, which
she named Thomas. Olivia's inner strength has always amazed me. No matter
what has come her way, her inner compass stays true north; she sets her goals
and accomplishes them.

Ella returned to Brooklyn, but like me, was barely able to get out of bed.
Fortunately, her law firm gave her some time off, which she needed. Then,
one day something clicked in her brain that made her realize she needed to
function. She promptly went to a dog shelter, rescued a Chihuahua named
Panda, and began walking outside every day, getting fresh air, and interacting
with others. I felt that things were beginning to get back on track for her. Then
she left her dream job and left New York. She and her husband moved to Los
Angeles, and later she left her husband. I was worried about her because she
seemed to be running from everything, but to what? Ella's independence is
matched only by her brilliance. She was a dynamic duo unto herself, but she
was still not completely herself.

One blustery morning, I was shoveling snow from my driveway when I received a call from Lisa Hennessy. My team had been chosen to participate in the following year's Eco-Challenge Fiji. Not two weeks earlier, I had considered selling all of my race gear, as it had been sitting unused in my gear shed. I started not only to cry, but also to shovel with purpose. It was the first real purpose I had had in three years.

I would be racing on Team Braveheart with an old teammate from Eco-Challenge Borneo who would be the team captain. Also on the team would be two rookies: Shane Habib, a stuntman from California who happened to have been good friends with Johnny, and a former Tour de France cyclist, Tyler Hamilton. I flew to Santa Barbara to meet and train with the two rookies for a weekend. Both men were funny, kind, and strong. We hiked in a beautiful canyon but were on full rattlesnake alert after Shane almost stepped on one. It was the first time in almost a year that I'd been on a bike when we rode Gibraltar—a long steep hill in the Santa Barbara hills. To say that I couldn't keep up would be an understatement; I had one speed on the uphill—slow. But on the downhill I was quick. That's where I caught up and sometimes passed them.

Not long after that weekend of training, we got a call from the team captain. He no longer wanted to race because he didn't want to finish the race in second place behind Mike Kloser's team. Mike is one of the strongest racers in adventure racing and usually wins. I was relieved that he didn't want to be captain, as I had memories of racing with him in Borneo. Every time his number came up on my phone, I'd get a stomachache. I knew we could cross the finish line with him but wanting to win when none of us had raced in at least a decade was a pipe dream. Plus, there were rookies on the team who had never competed in an adventure race. They were very capable, but realistically, there was no chance of our team winning. I just wanted to race and finish.

The upside of that team weekend was meeting Tyler. Tyler was truly one of the nicest, kindest human beings one could ever meet. He was incredibly calm and helpful with all things related to biking, without an ounce of arrogance.

After our training weekend, I bought and read his book. He was a professional road cyclist, and the only American rider to win one of the five monuments of cycling, taking Liège-Bastogne-Liège in 2003. I also learned that he could handle more pain than anyone I knew.

I was desperate to do this race; I knew I needed it for my own sanity. I contacted the race relations woman and asked if I could have the Braveheart team spot. She agreed if I could get her my teammates' names ASAP. I immediately called Tyler to see if he would race on the new team, as I knew his biking ability and pain tolerance. After what had gone down with the old team, he was no longer interested in adventure racing. To him, it sounded like an awful sport. Who can blame him? When you explain to two rookies that they should expect to lose at least twenty pounds, be awake for over forty hours, probably experience some degree of hypothermia, and that they may not have the energy to or be capable of walking, and may feel like they're starving, but have to suck it up and keep going—those aspects of adventure racing make it almost impossible for someone in their right mind to say yes.

Jason Middleton was our team advisor, and he tried to explain to them what they needed to do: "Limit the food you carry. Keep packs as light as possible to move faster."

"We need to carry more food," they responded.

"You can't," he countered.

Adventure racing is abusive, yet it's the most fun sport I've participated in. It's always hard explaining the "fun" part to people, especially after they've heard the abusive part.

I was fortunate that within forty-eight hours I had secured Harald Zundel, a former Navy SEAL with over two decades of racing experience. He was the man who saved my entire team from the cliff in Switzerland. The other two who signed onto my team were Blain Reeves, a former Army Ranger of the Year, and Guy LaRoque, a roofing contractor from Newport Beach,

California, who was a very strong cyclist. I envisioned him as being the Tyler Hamilton of the team.

The problem of having someone who is so strong in one area is that they probably lack in others. While Guy's strength on a bike was never in question, he had not done an adventure race in more than twenty years, and once we arrived in Fiji, that became very apparent.

When tasked with buying the team tarp, Guy pulled out the big heavy blue ones they sell at Home Depot. The look on the gear check person's face said it all. Thankfully, Blain and I had two extras with us that were lightweight. We had to carry both, but it was worth it not to carry what Guy brought.

Guy was also on a keto diet. Before the race, he wasn't shy about trying to get us to do it as well. He had boxes of bars that he had purchased for the race. I declined, as did Harald and Blain. I needed as much regular food, not to mention salt, sugar, carbs, and fat, as possible when racing. Diets don't work on a racecourse. He was low-energy within four hours.

The first discipline of the race was an all-day, most-of-the-night paddle to some islands off the coast. Guy begged us to put up the sail of our traditional Fijian canoe, even though there wasn't a hint of wind. We put the sail up twice to give him a break, only to watch ourselves go nowhere. Finally, Harald, navigating from the back of the boat, calmly said, "You have to suck it up and paddle."

The land portions of the race weren't any better for Guy. Stuffed with food, he didn't want to eat, his pack weighed more than everyone else's, and he didn't know the locations of items he'd packed. He carried three headlamps and was unable to find any of them. Knowing where everything is at all times is crucial. When Harald offered to carry his pack for him or to carry some of his load, Guy angrily responded, "Why, is there something wrong?"

"Yes, there is something wrong," I wanted to say. "You're slow. Harald and Blain have been carrying you for days." I held my words.

We all backed off at that point. We realized that Guy was not his normal self, and any negative comments were unproductive and pointless. Instead of sparking him to do better, they were irritating him. He would wander off trails by himself and wouldn't get out of the pools we had to swim through when the rest of us were back on the trail. The bike section started off just as badly. Within minutes of getting onto his bike, his "brand-new" shoes broke. As we all had extra pedals and Guy's tennis shoes were in his bike box, Blain took Guy back to the last checkpoint to get his shoes. Unfortunately, the truck with our bike boxes had already left. We duct-taped and zip-tied one shoe together. I knew it would be impossible for him to keep it on in the thick, muddy jungle hike and bike, but I didn't say a word.

Even though our team, Team Flying J, was named in honor of Johnny, I couldn't talk about him in any way without crying. I could only discuss him when my walls were up, I'd had ample sleep, and I was feeling emotionally strong. No one brought up his name unless I did first. My teammates were great that way. I tried not to think about him during the race—but then there were these crazy signs that let me know he was around on some unseen level. Strangely, that was the number one reason I wanted to race; I knew I'd experience him out there. On a long paddle down a river, I looked up at the moonlit sky and saw the Batman symbol in clouds backlit by the moon. I felt it was Johnny letting me know he was around, which was an awesome reassurance for me.

The night before the ropes section of the race, and the gnarly trek over moss-covered rocks to get there, we slept for a few hours and then left without breakfast. Our crew guy didn't wake up in time to make breakfast and, most importantly, coffee, for us, so I wasn't at my best when I started my day. We were falling all over the place on the sharp and slippery rocks. I was spent. I'd had no food, very little sleep, and again, no coffee. Before clipping into the long dangling ropes that we were about to ascend, a producer called me over and asked if she could speak to me.

She asked about Johnny. I said, "I can't," got up, and walked to the ropes. I floundered for an hour trying to move an inch, bawling my eyes out and berating myself. My guys patiently waited at the top for me. I was humiliated, embarrassed, and so sorry that I made them wait for me. They said not to worry, that it was no big deal. But it was to me.

We continued into the night. The freezing rain that fell, soaking every bit of our clothing, was relentless. In the glow of my headlamp, it looked like snow, which made it seem even more surreal, as we were in the middle of the jungle. I wondered how many of the racers the race directors were killing on the course. We spent more than a few hours commenting on what sadists they all were to be able to come up with a torturous course like this. Even though it had been almost two decades since the last Eco-Challenge, these people had not lost their touch.

I was going through the boulders, clipped in, rappelling and ascending, and getting colder and colder. It had stopped being a race and had become the proverbial every man for himself. It was a test of survival. Harald and Blain were up ahead of me, and Guy was somewhere behind me. We all knew the next checkpoint had a tarp we could get under, and our only goal at that moment was getting to the tarp. There was no other option. If any of us were to stop, we'd freeze to death, and we knew that a night rescue wasn't an option in that spot. We were so far apart from each other, and each of us realized that no one was coming back to find anyone. We were on our own individually, and I didn't know if we, as individuals, had the survival chops to make it through this.

Then I heard Johnny distinctly say, "Enough, Mom."

I excitedly responded with, "Hi!" I felt so comforted by his voice, his presence with me. I agreed with him wholeheartedly that this would be my last race. I would quit racing and finally be that social edict of a stay-at-home female. I vowed to learn to cook and bake. I made promises that I'd made over and over for more than twenty years. Then a surprising thought came into focus. Was Johnny in a place to lecture his mom about extreme sports? I didn't think so. He had inadvertently given me the push I needed to continue. I pressed on with the intent of reaching that tarp.

All of us made it to the tarp, where we spent a few hours shaking, but somewhat sheltered from the freezing rain. Guy was incoherent. We woke up the next morning in clothes that were still soaking wet to begin the swimming section. The water was so cold my skin felt like little needles were attacking it.

I was miserable, but so very alive. I tried not to smile. I loved it. On land, I followed in Harald's footsteps. Staying always one or two steps behind him allowed me to basically check out and just follow. Blain spent that entire section helping Guy get through it. Guy wasn't answering when asked how he was doing and got angry if someone tried to carry some of his weight. He was having a very difficult time and had been for days, yet he said nothing and carried on. I was growing very concerned about my friend.

While paddling down rapids in another boat section, he fell out of the boat and refused to get on his back facing downstream with his feet up, which is the standard position for a swimmer in rapids. "Turn around!" we yelled.

He was headed for a very large boulder. Since he had just finished his whitewater training a month or so before the race, he should have known this. His mind was just no longer capable of logically processing thought. His lethargy had caught up to him. His eyes were rolling into the back of his head. By the time we hit the exit point, we were past the dark zone pull-out time. I knew we'd pay a heavy time penalty for that.

We were now stuck in a small village because we couldn't cross the river at night. We stayed in the home of a couple who provided some great food, a warm room, and a bed and blankets for Guy. Harald, Blain, and I slept on the couches or the floor so Guy could get a much-needed, quality night of sleep— except that he refused to lie back and rest.

While the rest of us addressed our wounds, Guy just sat and stared. Whenever we asked how he was doing, the question was always met with a terse "Fine." We were helping each other with our various injuries and our tender feet, but Guy not only didn't ask for or accept help, he wouldn't help himself. His feet looked like hamburger meat when we finally saw them. Being on a team means not only helping your teammates, but also accepting help from them. No one likes to appear weak or to need help, but we have to rely on each other because if one person is out, the entire team is out.

Later, on another section of the course, late at night, we thought we were lost while stand-up paddle boarding (SUP) and decided to pull out of the river to let Guy rest. A farmer found us in his field and convinced us to get up and follow him. He showed us where the checkpoint was, and we were relieved that we were closer than we had thought. We had finally gotten off the water. We checked in at the checkpoint and were offered an unfinished house that provided a roof over our heads.

My dreams of a top-ten finish long given up, I would have happily accepted last place just to cross the finish line. If we went nonstop, we would be within twenty-four hours of the finish line. Blain arranged for a horse to carry Guy through the next jungle section, to the next and final camp, where our crew person waited for us with food and dry clothes. We decided to try to continue the next morning, after a good night's rest.

When we woke up, Guy was unable to stand. Blain got on his hands and knees so Guy could use him to crawl up and stand. All Guy had to do was stand up so we could get him onto the horse. After an hour of watching this, my dream of crossing the finish line in Johnny's name vanished.

I looked at Harald and whispered, "Should I call it?"
With no emotion he responded, "Yeah."

I got up and said, "Guy, you have one minute to get up." I knew I would appear as an unsympathetic bitch, but I wasn't going to let him jeopardize his health any further.

"I can't," he said.
"Okay. I'm calling it."

He argued with me that he didn't want to quit and pleaded that we give him more time. Blain offered to help him again.

I said, "No. You just spent an hour trying to help him." I looked back over to Guy and said, "You can tell all of your friends in the bar back in Newport Beach that your girl quit on you. I don't care. But this is ridiculous. No race is worth your leg."

I didn't fully understand the true danger of his situation. The cameraman knew; he had seen what Guy had hidden from us. One of his legs was twice the size of the other and bright red. He had urinated on himself during the night because it was too painful for him to stand. The insane thing was, he refused to quit. That's how mentally tough he was. Most people would have quit with the amount of pain he had to have been in. While I went to the person manning the checkpoint to inform him of our team's decision to quit, the cameraman radioed headquarters to bring in a helicopter for Guy and not send a car. The cameraman's decision most likely saved Guy's leg and quite possibly his life. Thank God for the cameraman.

Guy had turned septic and was very close to losing his leg. Had he gotten on that horse or taken the long car ride to the next checkpoint, he very easily could have lost more than his leg. Amazon Prime filmed it all.

Bear Grylls flew in for the rescue, loading Guy onto the helicopter for his flight to a hospital. Guy was transported to New Zealand, where he spent almost three weeks in the hospital while doctors worked hard to save his leg. The rest of us hung back at the village waiting for Bear to helicopter back for us. Once onboard, I told Bear that I had failed as a team captain by not speaking up and standing up to Guy pre-race. It was my fault for having him on the team and I vowed to make much better decisions for the next Eco-Challenge.

Bear seemed impressed that I was admitting a huge failure. A year's hopes and dreams were over and it was disheartening to return home without finishing the race.

While I didn't cross the finish line, I had found my old self again, and maybe a new understanding of leadership. I consoled myself that at least I got to be *on* the racecourse, that I was going home to my new home, another Park City flip, and home to my kids. I was mainly grateful that I had gotten the primary thing I had come for: I got to hear Johnny's voice.

Two days later, in a hotel room in Fiji, I wasn't feeling quite right. The doctors were in the room that Harald, Harald's angel of a wife, Susie, Blaine, and I were sharing. They were debriding Harald's leg with a hotel toothbrush. Susie was taking pictures, not at all worried or fussing over Harald because this is considered normal behavior when you're married to an athlete of his caliber. After a nice long shower, my legs felt too painful to walk. As I sat wrapped in a hotel robe, eating Tandoori chicken, I asked the doctors if they could have a look at me. They said I was fine.

In the middle of the night, I was hit hard with diarrhea and a very high fever. I texted my doctor in Park City and asked him to notify Global Rescue. By the next night, I was being flown in a private Global Rescue jet to a hospital in New Zealand.

Delirious with fever, I saw this very bright white light. Is this *the* light, I asked myself in disbelief as I focused on it? And then it instantly closed and went black. I deeply felt that something was telling me that I was meant to be here. For the first time in years, I was totally fine with being here, on Earth, for as long as I needed to be, and Johnny would wait for me on the other side.

Growing up Catholic, seeing my mom get shunned by the church for being divorced, and then attending any number of churches with my friends, I never knew where I really fell on the religious spectrum. I do know one hundred percent that I believe in God, the Universal, Creational energy. That faith has grown stronger since Johnny died. The book that was the most helpful to me was *Journey of Souls* by Michael Newton. It made sense out of all the different religions and helped me understand what Johnny was doing and where he was. I'd never had an explanation for the voice I've heard four times, which had saved me physically, but I knew it was a spiritual connection.

The first time I heard the voice, which was male in sound, but stronger than that, I thought I was hearing things. It was definitely not my own voice. This voice is clearly my protector. I heard it say "No" while in camp at the base of the Matterhorn. I was uncertain of the meaning, but I knew that I would eventually understand. Just below the summit, I could feel the irritation of my fellow climbers. I knew what the voice meant—it was time for me to quit, and I knew I was quitting because I'd heard that voice.

Race Across America in 2003 was another time I'd heard it. It was my turn to ride, and it was in the middle of the night on a windy country road with a steep descent. I was going well over forty mph. in the headlights of my chase car. The rules for racing in the dark were that, for safety, you had to stay within headlight distance of the car that followed you. Each team used their drivers and cars for this. Clear as could be, I heard the voice say, "Slow down."

What? This is what you dream of—speed. The goal is to place better, to finish the race, to not work so hard on the uphills. You never apply the brakes on a downhill. But I knew the voice and, although I wasn't sure why, I needed to slow down. I did as I was told. I learned why almost immediately—askew to the road, at the bottom of that hill just around a curve, were railroad tracks. Had I hit those tracks at the speed I was going on my skinny little tires, I would have flown over my handlebars. Okay, wow! *I will always listen,* I thought.

I'd also heard it while sorting family pictures in my garage. I had a stack of pictures of my former husband and Johnny in front of me and there was a trashcan within arm's reach. I had the thought to throw all of them away. No one would ever know.

The voice responded, "Then you'd be the asshole."

I told myself that I needed to keep my side of the sidewalk clean, that I couldn't and shouldn't control anyone but me, and what I said and did.

The fourth and last time I heard it was while mountain biking in Deer Valley, Utah. It was autumn and the single-track trail was covered in leaves. I was flying on a downhill section of the trail that curved in different directions. A protruding root grabbed my front tire and threw my bike sideways. I flew over the handlebars and heard the voice say, "Duck."

I did as instructed just as my shoulder, hip, and ankle—in that order—hit a tree. My ankle hit hard enough that it took a month to flex it again, and it was the third point of impact. Had I hit headfirst I probably wouldn't have survived the head trauma.

I have always thought it would be hard to climb big mountains without a belief in God. I find comfort in prayer and meditation. I know that Johnny is with God, and that gives me great solace. If he can't be here with me, I'm happy he is there with God.

Epilogue

Ben Jones, mountain guide, throwing some of Johnny's ashes off the summit of Mount Everest.

I knew the Triple Crown—Everest and her two sister peaks—were no longer on the table, but I wanted to take some of Johnny's ashes to the summit of Everest. He had always wanted to fly off that mountain and I wanted to make his wish a reality. The girls didn't want me to attempt the Triple Crown or even to return to Everest, even though the purpose was something that they supported. Availing her talent as an attorney, Ella presented her case, calmly asked me not to go, to instead stay home and celebrate her birthday with her and her friends in Park City. Olivia was more direct and said she would never speak to me again if I went. I had the feeling she meant it.

I asked God and Johnny for a sign. *Please let me know if I'm doing the right thing by going*, I asked them both. Within forty-eight hours, I had received a sign. I tore my ACL. A broken leg would have been a more definitive response, but I got the message. I could have probably managed the climb technically, but I knew I had received the message I had asked for.

I reached out to the guide, Ben Jones, and asked a favor. He agreed to take Johnny's ashes to the summit in a USC shot glass that was given to me by Eli Meyer, Kelly's son. Eli had purchased a beautiful, thick glass with USC in big red letters. Johnny loved shot glasses and he loved USC. It all seemed so fitting. I was disappointed that I wouldn't be setting Johnny's ashes free from the summit, but comforted by the fact that he would "fly" from the peak.

My daughters had no problem with me going to base camp, as long as the word "climb" was not involved. They knew I would be handing Johnny over to Ben and, approximately six weeks later, if all went well, he and Johnny would be on the summit. The girls were happy about that. So, with three friends, including Trevor's mom, Lynn, I made another appearance at the base of that magical mountain.

With tears in my eyes, I gave Ben the shot glass and Johnny's ashes. The next morning, my friends and I departed base camp via helicopter for our quick return to Kathmandu. I tried not to focus on the very real possibility that the team might not summit, and that Johnny wouldn't fly from the summit. I knew the outcome was something I had no control over, and set my mind to know that whatever happened was what needed to be.

At the beginning of the trek to base camp, I was really sad that I wouldn't be climbing. I was finally in great shape and felt strong. However, by the time I left base camp, the helicopter hovering and shuddering in the high altitude, I didn't even look back at her. I knew I had made the correct decision, not only for my daughters, but also for myself.

In an almost whiteout storm on the summit, Ben granted Johnny his wish to fly from the top of Mount Everest. When Ben emailed me to let me know, I was relieved and saddened. It should have been me up there with my son, yet I knew that my daughters needed me more. It was a complete repeat of how I felt about not going to Switzerland to bring Johnny home. My daughters' needs had to come first. They were alive, and they mattered to me as much as Johnny. I think surviving siblings can get lost in the death of their sibling. All of the focus goes onto the child who passed while the ones who remain struggle immensely. I tried to be aware of that. While I miss my son, every minute of every day, I know how fortunate I am to have these two beautiful humans in my life.

We couldn't place Johnny's ashes in only one location; there were too many places that he cherished on this planet. I sprinkled some in the water at Little Dume, his favorite beach. Kelly and I watched as they shimmered down through the dark blue water. Johnny has flown off the Grand Teton where my climbing mates, Forrest and Amy, watched in amazement as a falcon appeared out of nowhere as I threw his ashes from the summit. Ella started leaving his ashes whenever she ventured to a place she thought her brother might have liked. She has taken him to the Amazon, and he may or may not be on the fifty-yard line of a major football stadium. He is on the summit of Kilimanjaro, one of his favorite mountains. We tried to bring him to the places he traveled—except for the Grand Canyon, which was not a favorite locale—and loved. In my heart I knew he preferred being out in the world and not left on a shelf.

———

I routinely trained, raced, and climbed. On one climb, I awoke from a deep sleep, forced myself up, and walked straight to the coffee maker in the familiar Dow Villa motel room. I was back at Mount Whitney sharing a room with my daughter's then boyfriend. The night before, he had held court at a pizza parlor across the street from the motel. Most of the fifteen people at the table knew Johnny. It struck me as I sat there for the eleventh time, eating my pre-climb pizza, that I was still doing the same things I had enjoyed twenty years before. I was still a climber and an athlete. I had sacrificed my marriage and other relationships to satisfy the drive within me, and I knew that nothing short of severe physical injury would alter my choices. It's who I am; it's what I do.

As I thought about my choices, I realized my son had made similar socially acceptable sacrifices. Johnny chose wingsuiting over a life with a smart, funny, and gorgeous girlfriend and an unlimited future. I understood because I had, just like Johnny, chosen sports over important relationships. The only difference was that, while I limited the level of danger associated with my choices, he embraced the extreme of it. He continued to partake in a sport that he had to know would probably kill him. Once someone starts BASE jumping, the average life span is six years, and he was aware of those odds. Add a wingsuit to BASE jumping, and throw in the thrill of proximity flying, and the timeline for survival shrinks. He knew the percentages. He religiously studied the list of BASE jumping deaths and knew many who had passed.

Some time after his death, I visited a website that lists those who have passed in similar accidents. I wanted to see if Johnny's name was on it. Initially, I couldn't find his name and was angry that it wasn't listed. Then I scrolled down a bit and kept scrolling. When I finally saw his name quite a way down, I was shocked by how many others had died after him. As I read through the names, I thought of Johnny's words: "How can we fault someone for being who they are?"

I had to accept the consequences of Johnny's choices and passions because I, too, needed extreme sports in my life. I, and all who love Johnny, live with the ultimate result of his proclivities. I often reflect on unanswerable questions that fill my mind. *Did we lose Johnny because he was following in his parent's footsteps, or because he was always meant to be his own person and follow his dreams? Was he simply wired differently than most young people? Was he fortunate enough to be born into a family who not only participated in extreme sports, but supported him in his as well? Or was that a curse?*

There was no answer. Johnny, like me, knew the potentially risky outcome of what we elected to participate in and still accepted those challenges.

Every minute of every hour during the first few months after Johnny passed seemed excruciatingly slow and painful. I really didn't think the pain in my chest and the hollowness in my soul would ever go away. Thankfully, time softens the sharp edge of the pain of loss. Eventually the anxiety ceased and, while there are still small, unexpected bouts of extreme sadness, I've learned to live with Johnny's choices.

Looking back at those years after his passing, I catch myself wondering how I managed to get through it all. Sports and athletics were my passport to letting go of perpetual grief. Of course, my girls and my friends were amazingly supportive and helpful, but eventually I realized I had to do most of the work myself. I still fill the bird feeders to make certain that I'm outside in nature daily, because that's one of the times I feel connected to Johnny. I can sense that Johnny is with me when I'm outdoors. It's a place both of us loved and respected.

As time has gone by, I've learned to trust more in the signs that Johnny sends my way. I can feel his energy around me when I am in motion, skiing downhill fast or on my bike speeding down a trail. I feel his presence, and it feels like he is enjoying it almost as much as I am. I will never stop looking for signs from him. When I see a hawk soaring over my head, or when the lights flicker, I greet him with a smile and a heartfelt "Hi Johnny!" Whenever I see the number twenty-three, his number, I smile. His signs to me are endless, and for that, I'm grateful. I'm also thankful that I communicate with Johnny—even though he's not physically present, his spirit, soul, energy, or whatever you want to label it, is near. Gratitude has slowly replaced the darkness of sorrow and grown into appreciation for the time I was fortunate enough to have him in my life.

I found my missing mojo during the race in Fiji when I heard Johnny's voice, clear as a bell. His voice helped me understand that I shouldn't be focused on what is missing from my life, but instead engaged with all the wonderful aspects that I do have in my life.

In the midst of the long grief recovery process, we—his family and friends— created and contributed to various charitable organizations that Johnny was passionate about. He loved children, and we were determined to keep the energy of his humanitarian visions alive. Contributions were made to BlinkNow, a nonprofit organization that operates a globally recognized school and children's home in Surkhet, Nepal; the Cambodian Children's Fund, which assists children in one of the poorest areas of Phnom Penh; and the Johnny Strange Skatepark, the first skatepark in the Kingdom of Bhutan, which was built in Johnny's honor. Donations were also made to Simon's Rock, A Grannie Garden in Cambodia, and other charitable foundations. Scholarships were set up at Malibu High School, and Johnny's Adventure Reading Corner at Point Dume Marine Science Elementary School was introduced. His dad created the Johnny Strange Legacy Inspire Skate Program as a platform in partnership with the Boys and Girls Club of Malibu to honor his son.

Johnny was inspired by the world, by cultures, nature, and adventure. Our hope was that Johnny would continue to inspire people to push the limits of what they believe is possible. He knew that no matter where you came from or what you've been through, you can always keep climbing. He truly believed that, when you do the thing you fear the most, the death of fear is certain.

A documentary film crew began filming Johnny's adventures before he passed. It was released as *Johnny Strange: Born to Fly* and won the Malibu Film Festival in 2020. It was rereleased under the title *American Daredevil* in 2021.

The movie traces his incredible life and untimely death, and examines what it meant to Johnny to live life to the fullest. It's candid and delves into his adventures and records, including being the youngest person to parachute onto the North Pole and reach the Seven Summits. It illustrates the complex relationship between an extreme adventurer and danger and the almost narcotic-like addiction that manifests from it. Johnny lived by the axiom, "The day I let fear deter me from following my dreams, I have already died." Fear never interfered with his dreams.

The more I regained my emotional footing, the more I relied on sports as part of my support system. I continued to climb and race, including Racing the Planet in Sri Lanka, Climbing Mount Olympus four times, Mount Timpanogos three times, Mount Blanc twice, Gran Paradiso, Grand Teton twice, Cactus to Clouds, and Rim to Rim to Rim. I participated in Racing the Planet in Georgia, the Avalon 50 twice, climbed Kilimanjaro, and climbed Mount Whitney several times. I captained my team for Eco-Challenge Fiji, biked the Death Valley Century and Santa Barbara Century, and in Nepal, I trekked Mustang. I explored the Narrows in Zion National Park, canyoneered in Utah, paddled the Colorado River through the Grand Canyon three times, and took surf trips to Costa Rica and Hawaii.

I've learned that there's no better way for me to memorialize my son than to continue to participate in sports and adventures. I had, like anyone else who has lost a loved one, the option to live in pain or to affirm the life of the one who passed by living as fully and vibrantly as I could. I knew Johnny would not want me wrapped in sorrow for the rest of my days. He would want me to follow my heart, as he had. In the beginning, it feels like an impossible trail to navigate, but eventually one begins to feel more complete, and the wound to the heart and soul begins to heal.

Johnny and I are kindred spirits with a passion for extreme sports. Each adventure experience I had reinforced the feeling of being close to him. I recognize now that his energetic presence will be with me always, no matter what I'm doing, but I relish the idea that he's with me when I race or climb. I have no doubt that we will meet again and look forward to the time when we can laugh together about all of our exciting ventures, but mainly I want him to be proud of the life I lived after he died.

Acknowledgements

My eternal gratitude for Tara Sutphen, for providing the introduction to Devra Jacobs, my amazing and unflappable book agent who made this all happen, to Brenda Hayward for her photography skills, and to my co-author and most patient editor, Brit Elders. Thank you all for believing! Brenda Knight and Mango Publishing, I couldn't be happier working with such a great team.

To my family:

Fred and Otgo Farnham, Scott Matson, Tyson Matson, Stacia Matson (RIP), Linda Wells (RIP), Gladys Farnham (RIP), and my beautiful girls. I know it wasn't easy having a mom who did these sports. Thank you for your love, encouragement, and support.

I must acknowledge the incredible and amazing people I am so fortunate to know and call my friends.

To my friends:

Christina, Brian, Meghan, and Kayleigh (RIP) MacGregor, your friendship means the world to me. Sally and Mohsen DiBaei, Jacquelyn Zeman (RIP), Anthea Stiegler, Brenda and David Hayward, Tricia Middleton, Aiden Middleton, Camryn Middleton. My original workout girls: Debby Felman (RIP), Pam Litz, Tara Sutphen, Terry Wallace, Tonya McArthur, Marie Lehman, Peggy Fields, and Mary Miller Blakslee—thank you all for more verbal workouts than actual calorie burning.

Tracy, Skip, Jack, and Chelsea Murgatroyd, life wouldn't be the same without you. Mark Burnett, Roma Downey, Mimi Loving Hall, Little Dume Band— thank you for the amazing song, Brian, Karen, Rhett, and Aubrey Burgess,

Mary Gadams, Jerri Churchill, Frank Churchill, Kay Hughes, Dr. David
Frankle, Rosemarie Frankle, Christy Hilton, Eamon Harrington, Veronica
Brady, John Watkin, Stephanie Paige, Dr. David Katz, Susan and David Saul,
Dianne Burnett, James Burnett, Cameron Burnett, Jamie Steindorff, my other
daughter (you'll never get rid of me!), Kirby and Honoré Kotler, Christopher
Cortazzo, you are some of the kindest and most generous souls on this planet.

Ellen and Michel Shane, Gordon Janow, Craig Clunies-Ross, Judith
Guillmont, Melissa Racouillat, Tricia Stabile Small, Martha Quinn, Lynn
Jacob, Dr. Jill Ferguson, Jerry Jacob, Trevor Jacob, Mark Reader, Matt Rosado,
Patrick VanRoten, Jordan Jacob, Cynthia and Dana Christiaansen, Janice
Nikora, Julie Berk, Nicholas Kent, Susan Walters, Linden Ashby, Inez and Jim
McGee, Lisa Hennessey, Debbie Williams, Amy Mathre, Paul Hedman, Laura
Rosenthal, Laureen and Greg Sills, Matt Hanover, Deborah Buckinavage, Alix
Hartley, Traci Coulter, Gerald Abrams, Brian Celler, and last but not least,
Kelly Chapman Meyer for all the sports (willingly or not), parties, and wholly
inappropriate humor.

To my teammates and rope-mates:

Guy LaRoque, Blain Reeves, Harald Zundel, Susie Schmelzer, Lakpa Rita
Sherpa, Mingma Sherpa, Chewang Sherpa (RIP), Eric Murphy, Adrian Crane,
Jason Middleton, Mike Trisler, Jeffrey Buell, Ben Jones, Wally Berg, Charlie
Engle, Jason Thomas, Nick Moore, Julian Sands, Jose Luis Peralvo, Forrest
McCarthy, Amy Brennan-McCarthy, Jack Dunn, Vern Tejas, Mark Macy, and
Marshall Ulrich.

I have been blessed to have an abundance of supportive people in my life and
apologize for any omissions. To protect the privacy of certain individuals, a
few names have been changed.

And to my love, THD.

About the Authors

Dianette Wells

An elite member of the fewer than four hundred individuals who have climbed each of the Seven Summits, including Kilimanjaro, Vinson, Elbrus, Denali, Everest, Aconcagua, and Carstensz Pyramid. She has participated in four Eco-Challenges, raced over one hundred and fifty miles across various deserts, biked across America, and adventure-raced around the globe.

She is the proud mother of three, continues to climb and race, and just finished her twentieth home remodel.

Follow Dianette's exciting adventures at DianetteWells.com and through social media, or email her at DianetteAuthor@aol.com.

Brit Elders

An internationally published author, Brit focuses her research and work on nonfiction topics. She has written books, articles, and documentary films, and ghost-written and edited for others with a goal of learning something new from each project.

She is the CEO of ShirleyMacLaine.com, a position she's held since its inception. An advocate for naturopathic health and healthy eating, Brit has hosted radio programs and been a guest on radio and television in the US, as well as other countries. Find out more about Brit's work at BritElders.com.

Mango Publishing, established in 2014, publishes an eclectic list of books by diverse authors—both new and established voices—on topics ranging from business, personal growth, women's empowerment, LGBTQ studies, health, and spirituality to history, popular culture, time management, decluttering, lifestyle, mental wellness, aging, and sustainable living. We were named 2019 and 2020's #1 fastest growing independent publisher by Publishers Weekly. Our success is driven by our main goal, which is to publish high-quality books that will entertain readers as well as make a positive difference in their lives.

Our readers are our most important resource; we value your input, suggestions, and ideas. We'd love to hear from you—after all, we are publishing books for you!

Please stay in touch with us and follow us at:

Facebook: Mango Publishing
Twitter: @MangoPublishing
Instagram: @MangoPublishing
LinkedIn: Mango Publishing
Pinterest: Mango Publishing
Newsletter: mangopublishinggroup.com/newsletter

Join us on Mango's journey to reinvent publishing, one book at a time.

Printed in the USA
CPSIA information can be obtained
at www.ICGtesting.com
JSHW031909230524
63681JS00005B/8